NASCAR NOW

NASCAR NOW

BY TIMOTHY MILLER
AND STEVE MILTON

FIREFLY BOOKS

A FIREFLY BOOK

Published by Firefly Books Ltd. 2004

First printing

Publisher Cataloging-in-Publication Data (U.S.)

Miller, Timothy.
    NASCAR now / Timothy Miller and Steve Milton. –1st ed.
[160] p. : col. photos., col. maps ; cm.
Summary: Guide to NASCAR and stock car racing, including biographies of drivers, analysis of racing teams, history of stock car racing and famous track venues.
ISBN 1-55297-829-X (pbk.)
1. Stock car racing. 2. Automobile racing drivers.
3. NASCAR (Association). I. Milton, Steve. II. Title.
796.72 dc22   GV1029.9.S74M55 2004

Library and Archives Canada Cataloguing in Publication

Miller, Timothy, 1951-
    NASCAR now / Timothy Miller and Steve Milton.
ISBN 1-55297-829-X
    1. NASCAR (Association) 2. Stock car racing—United States. 3. Automobile racing drivers—United States. I. Milton, Steve II. Title.
GV1029.9.S74M54 2004   796.72'0973
C2004-903289-5

Published in the United States by
Firefly Books (U.S.) Inc.
P.O. Box 1338, Ellicott Station
Buffalo, New York 14205

Published in Canada by
Firefly Books Ltd.
66 Leek Crescent
Richmond Hill, Ontario L4B 1H1

Cover and interior design by Lind Design
Printed in Canada

CONTENTS

INTRODUCTION

Two of today's top drivers, Dale Earnhardt Jr. (No. 8) and Jeff Gordon (No. 24), during 2004 Daytona 500 practice. Jr. won the race and Gordon placed eighth.

From the beaches of Florida and the dusty dirt ovals of the Southern United States, NASCAR racing has experienced tremendous growth, not only as a professional sport, but as part of our lives.

Each weekend the hundreds of thousands of fans that pack the track, and millions more watching on television, witness the color, the noise and the excitement as dozens of sleek race cars and compelling drivers provide heart-stopping action in a competition like no other.

Over six million people attend NASCAR Cup races annually, with an estimated 275 million viewing the races on national broadcasts across the globe. Billions of dollars are invested in sponsorship and promotion, and licensed NASCAR merchandise tops $2 billion per year. Each of the 36 Nextel Cup events averages 186,000 spectators. One Cup race draws more fans than the Super Bowl, a World Series baseball game, and a National Basketball Association finals game combined.

Cup drivers are revered as folk heroes, and some have become idols on a national scale as part of the fabric of society. Driver rivalries are intense, as is the competition between auto manufacturers.

When compared to other major league sports, NASCAR races are unique in presentation. Each race stands on its own as a major event with its own sense of urgency and impor-

tance, not unlike a playoff game in another sport. There is only one Cup race per week, so there's only one opportunity to view the race, and a concentrated effort is made to get the most from each weekly event.

NASCAR's stock car racing has grown to unprecedented levels. The vision that Bill France saw back in 1949 has, through hard work and sound business acumen, seen huge expansion over the past five decades, and this vision has continued through the efforts of his son, Bill Jr., and now grandson Brian who is taking NASCAR racing to the next stage of sports entertainment.

NASCAR Now covers the entire spectrum of this engrossing sport, from the beginnings to the present action-packed season. Along with a history of the sport, you will learn about some of the colorful personalities that helped make NASCAR what it is today. You'll follow the evolution of the NASCAR stock car, including the latest in safety technology, and learn more about the tracks and how the drivers win points, as well as the marketing machine that has fueled the sport. You'll discover the action and function of the pit stops, and will read about some of the hottest and most influential drivers of the present NASCAR scene.

So get buckled up and press that starter. It's time for the green flag.

In 1959, Lee Petty took home $19,050 for winning the inaugural Daytona 500. The 2004 winner of the same race, on the same track, was Dale Earnhardt Jr. He took home $1.6 million.

HISTORY

Curtis Turner and his Ford convertible at Daytona Beach. The soft-top division ran for several years in the late 1950s.

The real roots of stock car racing go back about 100 years with the introduction of the automobile.

Motoring contests were held in Europe and North America during the auto's formative years, but the contests were quite different in makeup on each side of the Atlantic Ocean.

European and British racing was performed on local roads and thoroughfares, evolving into road racing. Spectators lined streets and country roads as the cars roared past them only feet away. Eventually this road racing was curtailed with the advent of specially designed and constructed circuits that continue to this day.

In North America, road racing was the mainstay of early competition, but automobiles were expensive, and those who raced were usually wealthy sportsmen. By 1910, with the help of Ford's Model T, automobiles were more affordable to the masses and anyone with a competitive spirit could go racing.

But where to race? Aside from populated areas in the eastern United States most roads were nothing more than wagon paths, and extensive auto travel was virtually impossible. So races were held at county fairgrounds, where there were nice, smooth, oval-shaped horse-racing tracks.

By World War I, racing on these mostly dirt ovals had become very popular. Carl Fisher's 2.5-mile brick-paved oval just outside of Indianapolis, built in 1909 (now Indianapolis

Motor Speedway), took racing to new levels. A multitude of wooden-surfaced board tracks, a successor to bicycle velodromes, surfaced across the country over the next 20 years.

Soon the cars that raced on the board and dirt tracks became pure racing machines. At first the cars were basically larger automobiles, such as Mercedes-Benz, Hudson or Stutz roadsters with the fenders removed. By 1930, the forerunner of today's Indy-style car, the Duesenberg and Miller, dominated American racing.

While the Indy-style roadster developed through the 1930s – benefiting from national sanctioning by the Contest Board of the American Automobile Association (AAA) – smaller versions of these cars, including Sprint and Midget cars, plied the local fairgrounds, especially in the Northeast and Midwest United States.

A movement was also taking place in the South. In an effort to outrun government agents with cars full of illegally made whiskey, "moonshine" runners were modifying stock street cars and becoming quite successful at delivering the goods. The car of choice was usually the light, nimble and fast V8-powered Ford.

Soon the moonshine runners wanted to apply their driving talents against each other, so informal contests started, usually on a hastily built dirt oval in a farm field. As these impromptu contests grew and became popular, family and friends would appear to watch the bragging rights. Bleachers were built, hot dogs sold and prize money awarded.

To the north, full-fendered stock car racing, known as "jalopy" or "Modified" racing, was a mainstay on the ovals along with the AAA Indy-type cars, but these "stock" cars were far from stock with their modified engines, suspensions and cut-down bodywork. The cars of the South were more stock-like in appearance.

At this time, however, there was no unity with all the racers and tracks. Each track had its own set of rules and car specs. There was no overall governing body like the AAA's Contest Board.

Enter Bill France. An auto mechanic from the Washington D.C. area, France moved to

A minor altercation during a Modified race at Daytona Beach in the early years. All Fords, all coupes.

Daytona Beach on Florida's east coast in 1934 and set up shop. He raced his Modified in Florida and successfully promoted some small beach/road events at Daytona, but by the end of World War II he was thinking about a national sanctioning body that could oversee this type of racing. The AAA wasn't interested in racing cars that looked like anything you could drive off a car lot.

After meetings with other promoters, car owners and drivers just before Christmas of 1947, the foundations were laid, and in February 1948 the National Association for Stock Car Auto Racing (NASCAR) was legally incorporated.

For the first two years of its existence, NASCAR ran only a Modified class, but France believed if fans could identify with the cars on the tracks, they would bond with the sport. In 1949, France's vision and hard work came to life with NASCAR's new Strictly Stock division. Organized stock car racing was born.

The first race in this class was held in June 1949 at the new three-quarter mile Charlotte, N.C., dirt track (now Charlotte Speedway). With a purse of $2,000 and 13,000 fans to witness the event, this first race displayed that France meant business.

Although Glenn Dunnaway was the first to complete the 200-lap event, officials disqualified him as his Ford was running with illegal

Daytona Beach in 1957, with a large crowd waiting for the beach/road race to begin.

rear springs. So the first winner of a NASCAR stock car race was Jim Roper in his '49 Lincoln.

In 1950, the first NASCAR-based speedway opened, the 1.25-mile Darlington Raceway in South Carolina, with the first of many Southern 500 races.

In the early 1950s, NASCAR expanded from its southern roots to travel west to California and Arizona, and north to Michigan. The showroom stock cars became less and less showroom in appearance and performance, sporting the largest engines available, more safety equipment and heavy-duty brakes and suspensions.

As the decade progressed, more racetracks were built – substantial facilities with seating and amenities approaching that of baseball parks. As the sport grew, newly built tracks were all paved.

Stock car racing reached a level of maturity in 1959 with the opening of the Daytona International Speedway. The brainchild of Bill France, this 2.5-mile-long oval with 31-degree corner banking was constructed on 480 acres of northern Florida land. The track was built to replace the 4.1-mile oval-shaped beach/road course that NASCAR ran on the Atlantic shore in February.

After driving and watching races on the usual small dirt bullrings, the vast vista of the Daytona oval left drivers and fans alike goggle-eyed on their first visit.

The racers took to this new track right away. Cotton Owens set the pace in a Pontiac with a top qualifying speed of over 143 miles per hour. And in a photo finish that decided the inaugural Daytona 500 race victor some days later, Lee Petty, in a '59 Oldsmobile, was declared the winner over Johnny Beauchamp and his Thunderbird who originally took the checkered flag.

Starting in the early 1960s, NASCAR acquired many new fans as some of its events were televised. The sport grew in popularity and professionalism, and it became big business with the involvement of corporate sponsorship. A new generation of drivers emerged, drivers with no concerns about their pasts. Car manufacturers built cars specifically with winning races in mind. Tire companies devoted personnel exclusively to race car research and development. While this expansion took place, Bill France ran NASCAR with a firm hand.

At this time, one driver more than any other allowed NASCAR to flourish, and that driver was Richard Petty. This dark-haired, lanky second-generation driver from North Carolina started his career in 1958, and until his retirement in 1992, became the undisputed "King" of stock car racing. Many of his accomplishments will never be equaled. Some of his records include the most wins (200), most pole positions (127) and most consecutive wins (10 in 1967).

An immensely popular driver, Petty and his series of Plymouths became the sport's top ambassador. He spent almost as much time at the track signing autographs for his fans as he did behind the wheel. He is probably the most interviewed personality in any sport, and always gave back to the sport what he accomplished over his 35 years of racing.

In addition to NASCAR, another racing body was also involved in stock car racing during this time. When the AAA dropped its involvement with auto racing in 1955, the United States Auto Club (USAC) was formed, and it became the sanctioning body for most open-wheeled racing, including Sprint, Midget and Champ (Indy) car events.

USAC also had a stock car series, and was prominent in areas other than the Southern U.S. Although the USAC stock car series did not race as often as NASCAR, it provided some fierce competition with a lot of "box office" drivers of the day – drivers that were well-known from racing the Champ cars at tracks such as Pocono, Milwaukee and, of course, Indy.

Some of the more prominent USAC competitors were household names. Drivers such as A. J. Foyt, Mario Andretti and Parnelli Jones all raced stock cars on the USAC circuit along

Same race seven years later. No more rooster tails in the sand now as the Fords, Pontiacs and Mercurys take to the 2.5-mile tri-oval for the Daytona 500.

Fights between drivers were not uncommon, but they were never before a live television audience when CBS broadcast the Daytona 500 in 1979. During the final stages of this race, the first to go before a national live audience, Donnie Allison (No. 1) and Cale Yarborough (No. 11) tussled on the final lap while Allison was in the lead, and both cars ended up parked on the infield. Words between the drivers were traded, and then punches as Donnie (left), and then his brother Bobby (with helmet on) tag-teamed on Yarborough (right). Just good ol' boys exchanging views, something that would not be tolerated today. By the way, Richard Petty won the race, the fight was a draw and a lot more people turned on their televisions for the next race.

with piloting the open-wheel Champ cars. There were several stock-car-only drivers who could, and did, drive as well as anyone in NASCAR racing. Norm Nelson, Don White and Paul Goldsmith were just some of USAC's "regulars."

By 1970, however, there was a lot of internal strife at USAC, and its stock division fell to the wayside. While USAC continued with open-wheeled racing, the Indy-car series was taken over by Championship Auto Racing Teams (CART) in 1979. USAC is still a sanctioning body for Sprint and Midget competitions, as well as a dirt track Late Model Series.

In 1971, NASCAR entered what is considered its "modern" era. Tobacco giant R. J. Reynolds gave its financial support to NASCAR's top division, and the Winston Cup was born, a relationship that grew and prospered until 2003.

Also at this time, television started taking an active role in presenting Winston Cup races, starting with ABC's Wide World of Sports broadcasts. With this new exposure, large corporations such as Coca-Cola, Procter & Gamble and STP began to see the potential benefit of being financially involved in racing.

In 1979, the Daytona 500 was the first race to be televised live in its entirety. An estimated 20 million viewers watched Petty win the 500 as late-race leaders Cale Yarborough and Bobby Allison collided on the last lap, got out of their cars and started fighting while Petty took the checkered flag. All of this race action and drama, on and off the track, unfolded in front of millions of viewers and gave NASCAR a

tremendous boost in popularity.

In the early 1980s, with the advent of Detroit producing smaller, more fuel-efficient automobiles, NASCAR followed suit, and race cars were "downsized" with wheelbases of 110 inches for the new sedans.

Also at this time, new drivers were making their mark in Winston Cup competition. The most prominent were Dale Earnhardt, Darrell Waltrip and Bill Elliott.

Earnhardt, a second-generation driver, was one of the sport's most controversial figures. He ran with a fearless intensity, never holding back, and earned the name "The Intimidator." This North Carolina native also won the NASCAR championship seven times before his untimely racing death at the 2001 Daytona 500.

Waltrip, a brash newcomer from Tennessee, felt he could oust the veterans and was quite vocal about his plan. "Jaws" (as he was called early in his career) accomplished what he said he would, breaking the older drivers' monopoly on the sport by winning the title in 1981, 1982, and 1985. He raced until 1996 and is now one of the sport's broadcast personalities.

After a relatively slow start in racing in the late 1970s, Georgia's Bill Elliott would personify Winston Cup racing in the 1980s. He progressed through the ranks, winning the championship in 1988. Elliott earned fame by capturing the Winston Million – an award of $1 million for winning three of NASCAR's four biggest races. By winning the Daytona 500, the Winston 500 and the Southern 500 in 1985, Elliott became known as "Million Dollar Bill"

and "Awesome Bill from Dawsonville." Elliott continues to race in NASCAR's top division.

One of the most controversial changes in stock car racing at the NASCAR level took place in 1987. With the ever-increasing speeds, safety became an important issue, and NASCAR instituted the "restrictor plates," a device between the race car engine's carburetor and intake manifold. This plate reduces the fuel/air mixture in the engine, reducing engine power, hence reducing car speed. These devices are mandatory on the larger superspeedways like Daytona and Talladega.

Other safety developments have been instituted in the past few years, including roof flaps to reduce the possibility of cars becoming airborne, pit road rules and reduced pit lane speeds, and crash-absorbing barrier walls.

NASCAR has also expanded its track horizons over the past several years, replacing older, smaller tracks with new facilities such as Fontana and Texas to hold the legions of fans. Two road racing circuits are now part of the 36-race schedule. Watkins Glen and Sears Point give Cup teams a whole new outlook on racing the traditional oval-track cars.

Growth in NASCAR took a big step forward in August 1994, when the first Cup race was held at the Indianapolis Motor Speedway, the first race ever to be run at Indy aside from the Indy 500 Memorial Day classic held since 1911. Winning the inaugural Brickyard 400 at Indy was a young Jeff Gordon, who would go on to capture the 1995 Winston Cup title.

Gordon is one of the new breed of NASCAR stars who continues to dominate the sport to this day. While older drivers such as Terry Labonte, Rusty Wallace and Ken Schrader continue to race, younger drivers such as Gordon, Matt Kenseth and Tony Stewart exemplify NASCAR's current driving superstars.

The biggest recent change to NASCAR came at the end of the 2003 season. After a 32-year relationship, tobacco giant R. J. Reynolds relinquished the title sponsorship of NASCAR's premier stock car series. Based in Reston, Va., the wireless technology company Nextel Communications has partnered with NASCAR in presenting the top series, now called the Nextel Cup. This is a 10-year deal that began at the start of the 2004 season.

With Nextel's involvement, NASCAR's top stock car series has acquired its fourth name. In 1949, NASCAR's first year, the stock car series was known as the Strictly Stock division to differentiate it from the Modified and Roadster classes. In 1950, the stock class became known as the Grand National and remained the name of the top class until 1970.

In 1971, R. J. Reynolds (under its Winston brand) teamed up with NASCAR, and the races were known as the Winston Cup Grand National events until 1986 when the "Grand National" designation was dropped. NASCAR has kept the Grand National name for its feeder stock car series, combining the Busch North Series and the Winston West Series into one entity that is now known as the NASCAR Grand National.

STOCK CARS

Robbie Gordon at speed ahead of 2003 champ Matt Kenseth. This shot exemplifies the speed, color and dynamic of stock car racing.

In the early years, a racer could literally go to an auto dealership, buy a car off the lot and go stock car racing. The earliest NASCAR stocks were usually the lightest, most powerful cars in a manufacturer's line of two-door sedans. Popular entries around 1950 were the Oldsmobile 88, with its recently introduced overhead valve engine, or Chrysler with its state-of-the-art Hemi-head engine from 1951.

These cars were heavy, and while a car's engine would last, other parts such as the suspension, brakes and drive train failed much of the time. One of the biggest trouble spots was in the tires. Not only were they skinny compared to today's tires, they were stock road

tires, not built to withstand the excessive heat build-up, so blow-outs were very common.

In 1948, Hudson introduced its "Step-down" model, a bulbous vehicle with a wide stance and frame rails outside the rear wheels. Not only did this car sit lower than others, it offered superior handling characteristics for its day, and was very rugged.

Hudson did not have a V8 engine, but the carmaker did have an engineering department that saw the promotional value of stock car racing. When pioneer driver Marshall Teague came knocking at Hudson's Detroit plant, engineers worked with Teague to build a strong, dependable car. With its optional Hornet X7 engine, and special "export only" suspension

and brake package, the Hudson was a hard car to beat on the track in the early 1950s with its beefed-up axles, wheels and suspension equipment.

Other car manufacturers weren't going to sit around and let this six-cylinder upstart take all the prizes. Soon all makes were producing "export" brakes and suspensions, and with their more powerful V8 engines, Hudson's day was over by 1954.

The powerful Chrysler 300s dominated the tracks in the mid-50s, but the Big Three automakers, especially Chevrolet, had developed light, high-revving V8 engines that left the bigger, heavier cars in the dust. By 1960, Oldsmobile and Pontiac, each with its own engine, ran successfully with the Fords, Dodges and Chevrolets.

While engine development flourished in NASCAR's first decade, the cars became less and less like the "stock" cars they were to represent. The cars were still full-framed, but strengthened. The biggest brakes, wheels and suspensions were installed along with huge radiators. Four-speed transmissions were the norm. Body-wise, the cars became harder to tell apart from their street brethren. Bumpers were retained, but all trim and lights were removed. The glitzy and space-age look of stock dashboards gave way to a home-built

panel with aftermarket gauges and switches. The interior was gutted, replaced with metal panels, one racing seat and roll-bar protection.

Driver safety was slow to evolve. All glass except for the windshield was removed, single roll bars were replaced with cages and padding was installed around the roll bars. There were no safety fuel cells in the early years. Eventually tire manufacturers developed racing-only tires – tires with wide profiles that could withstand the high-heat, high-stress punishment – but tire failure was still common.

As domestic cars changed from 1960 to about 1990, stock cars changed in regard to Detroit's yearly model turnover. NASCAR strictly controlled the horsepower race of the mid-1960s when engines such as Chrysler's 426-cubic-inch Hemi and Ford's overhead camshaft 427 appeared, and eventually prohibited their use. Wind-cheating body styles such as the Ford Torino and Dodge Charger became prominent, and were naturals for the super-speedway with their 200-plus mile-per-hour speeds. Full-size cars such as the Ford Galaxie and Chevrolet Impala were replaced by mid-sized cars with a shorter wheel base, such as the Chevrolet Monte Carlo, Buick Regal and Ford Thunderbird.

By 1990, Detroit did not offer a V8-powered, rear-wheel drive car suitable as a basis for

The work never stops. Here, Jeff Gordon's crew works on the DuPont Chevy in the pit garage.

NASCAR Cup racing. While some elements such as the carburetor-fueled V8 engine, four-speed transmission and rear-wheel drive remain to this day, the cars on today's speedways have little more than the name in common with today's street-driven, front-wheel drive, V6-powered sedans.

Today's NASCAR Car

The NASCAR Nextel Cup car of today blends the reliability and power of a V8 engine with a solid, full frame and the most aerodynamic body that the rules will allow. This package has been developed not only for winning, but to offer the utmost in safety.

Engines

Power plants are custom-made by several racing engine manufacturers with very few factory parts. Each piece of each engine is built with endurance in mind, along with getting the most power. The engine block uses special alloys to provide more strength in key areas such as the main bearings. Cylinder heads are made of aluminum for light weight and valve porting versatility, which allows the engine to breathe better, thus providing more power.

Presently there are three engines in the top levels of stock car racing, from Ford, Chevrolet and Dodge. The displacement of these engines is 358 cubic inches, and they produce 750–800 horsepower, running high-octane gasoline through a huge carburetor. No fuel injection is allowed, and compression ratios are 12:1, much higher than a street car with a ratio of anywhere from 8:1 to 9.5:1.

All of these specialized engine parts allow a Nextel Cup car engine to withstand at least 8,000 rpm for hours at a time. Engines cost upwards of $40,000 each. They are hand-assembled then run on a dynamometer, a calibration machine which provides mechanics and engineers with every aspect of an engine's behavior.

The most significant, and one of the most controversial changes to NASCAR engines has been the use of a restrictor plate to slow down

This car lot from the mid-1950s shows Cadillacs, Oldsmobiles and Mercurys, among other Detroit iron. Take off the hubcaps, put in a roll bar, stick a number on the side and you could go racing in just about any of these cars.

Right: Tire man gets ready for a tire change from the early 1970s. Airguns are still the tool of choice. Note the knee pads.

Body

Car bodies are based on North American–made full-sized passenger sedans and have to look something like the models driven on the street. A body designation may be no more than three years old.

A car's frame consists of round and square tubing, with the roll cage making up an integral part. The frame is designed in three sections: the front clip, the driver's compartment and the rear clip. The front and rear clips are collapsible, and are intended to crush upon impact. The front clip is designed to push the engine down and out of the bottom of the car rather than back into the driver's area.

The body building process is determined by NASCAR rules and must meet 30 designated contours as set out in official guidelines. Tolerances are tight, allowing for differentials between the official templates and the car body of only 0.5–0.07 inches, depending on the area of the car being checked.

Several manufacturer's production panels, such as the roof and windshield posts, along with hoods, trunk lids and floor pans are used to build a race car body. Other areas such as the nose, tail and rocker panel sections are plastic and come from after-market firms.

The fenders, doors and quarter panels are hand-formed in the race car shop and worked on until they match the regulation templates. Only sheet metal is allowed – no aluminum or fiberglass can be used.

When the body has been fitted to the chassis, all body parts are then welded together and smoothed out into one seamless piece. This allows for better aerodynamic flow. The body is then primed, painted and lettered.

A stock car's windshield is made of a polycarbonate material called Lexan. It is strong but resilient and does not shatter. If an object is thrown up into the windshield, it will just scratch, dent or imbed itself there.

Race cars have had spoilers on their bodies for decades. This panel, along with a front-end air dam, is used to create downforce to help keep the car's stance on the track and improve traction.

the cars. This plate is sandwiched between the carburetor and intake manifold, controlling the fuel/air flow mixture into the engine.

The four barrels of a Cup carburetor measure $1\frac{9}{16}$ inches in diameter. The restrictor plate has four holes, each $\frac{29}{32}$ inches in diameter, blocking some of the carburetor's larger holes. This prevents the engine from taking in as much fuel, thus reducing the horsepower.

Restrictor plates became mandatory at the Talladega and Daytona superspeedways in 1988 in an attempt to slow the cars down after some high-speed accidents. Some believe if restrictor plates were not used, Cup cars could achieve speeds of at least 225 miles per hour on the larger tracks due to improved aerodynamics of the cars over the past decade.

Officials contend that restrictor plates help avoid high-speed crashes, but drivers complain that the plate causes multi-car pile-ups, as all cars are now so evenly matched that they race around the track in a tight group at 190 miles per hour. If one of these cars in a group loses control, blows a tire or engine, it usually causes a chain reaction and takes out other racers.

Kurt Busch's Ford gets some body work at Darlington, 2004. The team sponsor is quite obvious, but that's where the money comes from.

Right: Casey Mears (center) and the rest of the Target crew check out the tires for his Ganassi Racing Dodge during Daytona 500 practice, 2004.

In 1994, NASCAR introduced the roof flap, a safety device designed to keep a car from becoming airborne. Previously, at high speeds a car could fly into the air if it rotated during its spin, resulting in some horrendous crashes. The roof flaps disrupt the air flow, keeping the car close to the ground.

Through wind tunnel testing, these two flaps are recessed into the rear area of the roof. When a car reaches an angle of significant lift, the low pressure above the flaps sucks them open. The first flap is designed to open at a 140-degree angle from a car's centerline, and the second flap at a 180-degree angle to ensure the air flow is curtailed as the car rotates.

Fuel tanks

Bursting fuel tanks and fires were common in NASCAR's early years, resulting in driver deaths and serious injury. Today's 22-gallon tanks, known as fuel cells, have built-in features minimizing ruptures and explosions.

A fuel cell is a product of aerospace technology. It consists of a metal box centered in the car's rear and anchored with four strong braces. Inside the steel outer layer is a flexible, tear-

resistant bladder and foam baffling.

The foam reduces fuel sloshing around in the tank. It also reduces the amount of air in the cell which lessens the chance of explosion. If the cell does ignite internally, the foam absorbs the explosion. The car also has check valves that shut off the fuel supply if the engine is separated from the car.

Tires

Of all components on a race car, the tires are probably the most different from those on a regular passenger car. Race car tires are black and have a radial design, but that's about it for similarities.

A race car tire is about 12 inches wide and treadless. Both of these characteristics provide more traction and grip on the paved racing surface. The tires are built exclusively for racing, cost about $350 each and last 75 to 100 miles, on average. They are sticky to the touch – offering a better grip – and weigh less than street car tires.

Race car tires are filled with nitrogen, not air, because compressed nitrogen contains less moisture than compressed air. As heat builds in a tire, moisture in the tire evaporates and expands, causing the tire pressure to increase. Even a small amount of pressure difference will affect a car's handling capabilities. By using nitrogen, race teams have more control over pressure build-up.

Mike Skinner hastily exits his expired car at Darlington in 1999. Fires are rare in today's racing.

Dale Earnhardt Jr. all buckled in and ready to go, Las Vegas, 2004. Drivers don enough safety equipment to match jet fighter pilots. There are no ejection seats yet, though.

On racetracks longer than one mile, NASCAR rules require tires to contain an inner liner as a safety precaution. This inner tire is essentially a second tire mounted on the wheel inside the regular tire, and it allows the driver better control on the still-intact inner tire if the outer one blows during a race.

The material used in making the tire – its compound – is different for each racetrack. Softer compounds provide a better grip, but they wear out quicker than harder compounds. NASCAR, along with tire company engineers, have studied and determined suitable compounds for each racing venue, which depends on track surface and abrasiveness, number of turns and banking degrees of those turns.

A tire used on a road course, where the car must turn both left and right, will be different from a tire used on an oval short track with only tight left-hand corners.

Driver's compartment

Everything inside the driver's compartment has a purpose. There are no frills or luxuries in this cocoon of roll bars, padding and painted sheet metal.

First and foremost, a stock car's interior is constructed for safety. The roll cage is built from heavy tubing and is an integral part of the car. It can withstand severe punishment and is a testament to the dedication of safety rules in racing. A car may be involved in a severe mishap, such as hitting a retaining wall, getting jostled around with other cars or flipping over several times, but the driver is insulated within this strong cage and usually walks away.

There are other items inside the car which help keep the driver safe. The driver's seat is designed and manufactured to keep the driver within the car's roll cage and from hitting anything during a crash. The seat is almost an extension of the driver, and is molded to the body to fit like a glove. The seat will also absorb some of a crash's energy by bending upon impact.

Seats are formed to wrap around a driver's ribcage, and some newer seats wrap around the driver's shoulders as well. With the seat wrapped tightly around the ribcage, it provides greater support in a crash, spreading the load over the entire ribcage rather than concentrating on a small area. Aside from the rib and shoulder supports, seats have head supports on their right side, which gives the driver's head and neck a solid brace when going around left-handed corners for hours at a time.

The seat belt system is much more complex and robust than the unit in the average street car. The five-point harness restraint is designed

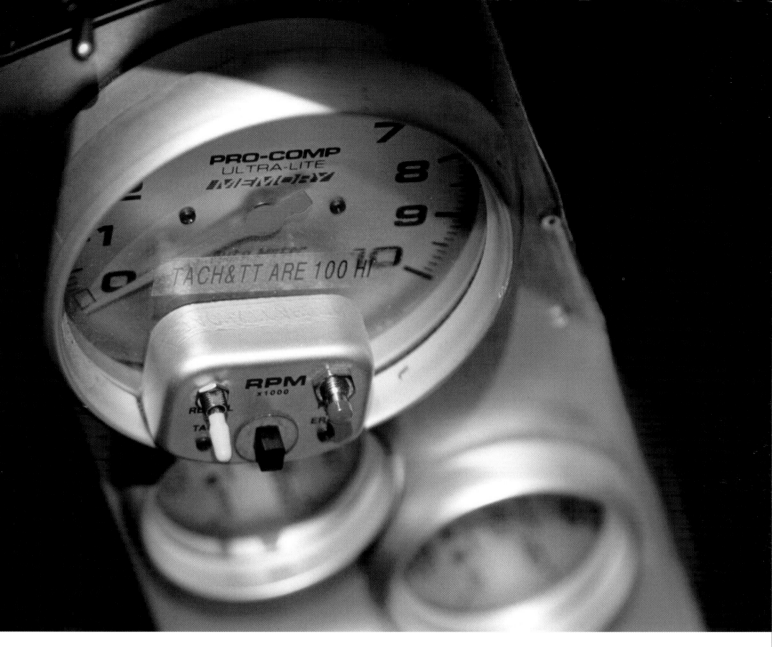

to hold the driver tightly in the seat so movement is restricted to the motion of the car. Made of thick padded webbing, the harness attaches at a central point in the driver's lap. Two straps come down over the driver's shoulders, two straps come around the waist and one comes up between the legs.

As race cars became more sophisticated over the years, window glass was taken from the car for weight and safety purposes. This led to some great air flow into the interior, but if the car was involved in a crash, especially a rollover, the driver's arms could flail out the door opening. Window nets, made of a nylon mesh webbing, were mandated, and this safety device covers the driver-side window opening to keep

the racer's arms inside the car in the event of an accident.

With no doors on a race car, a driver climbs into the cockpit through the driver's window area. As the driver sits in the seat, the steering wheel is fastened to the collapsible steering column. The wheel is removable for ease of entry and exit.

Inside the car, there is no padded dashboard with chrome trim and name plates. Instead, there are several toggle switches and instruments on a flat, homemade panel. No keys are needed to start this car. With a flip of the ignition switch and a press on the starter button, the engine roars to life. There are other switches on the panel, as well, including one that turns

One of the driver's best friends, the tachometer, situated in the cockpit with a commanding presence to show the car's engine speed.

That's racing. Dale Earnhardt Jr.'s Chevy displays the result of some close action with a competitor.

on a fan to cool the rear brakes when necessary, one to turn on the radiator fan when needed and another to turn on the blower fan that sends outside air into the driver's area.

There are no speedometers in race cars. The oil pressure gauge will show a reading of 70–80 psi (pounds per square inch) if the engine is running well at speed, and the oil temperature gauge will register 250°F to 270°F. Under good conditions, the water temperature gauge will read 190°F to 210°F and, like a street car, if the gauge reads over 220°F there's a problem in the cooling system.

A stock car does not have a fuel level gauge, but it has a fuel pressure gauge, which is a diagnostic-type unit that shows any irregularities in fuel delivery from the fuel cell to the engine. The ideal pressure is 7 or 8 psi.

Other gauges include a voltmeter, which displays the car's electrical charging system, and works like a street car voltmeter. If the needle is reading only 9 volts with a 12-volt battery system, then the alternator or other electrical device is faulty, and the battery will eventually go flat. Completing the gauge package is the tachometer, an instrument which displays the engine speed in revolutions per minute.

When at speed on a track, drivers use their experience and instinct about engine speed to shift gears. But with no speedometer, and speed limits imposed on entering and leaving the pit road, the driver will note his RPMs to keep his speed within these limits.

SAFETY

The basic premise of an auto race is simple: Win the race. Also uppermost in racing today is safety. Drivers and cars are subjected to punishment that not only destroys cars but could lead to serious driver injury and death if not for the safety equipment in place on the car, on the driver himself and on the racetrack.

Aside from the vaultlike safety of a race car's roll cage, driving suit and restraint system, the driver is protected in other ways.

Driver equipment

A stock car driver is sheltered from head to toe before taking to the track. Drivers don several pieces of protective gear that could save their

lives if an accident were to occur.

The head is the most vulnerable part of the body. As in other sports, the competitor's helmet is designed to dissipate impact energy and prevent outside elements from puncturing it. Attached to the front of the helmet is a full face shield, protecting the eyes.

A racing helmet is comprised of three parts: the outer shell, the outer liner and the inner liner. The outer shell is made from gel coat, special resins, carbon and substances such as Kevlar, providing an extremely hard and durable surface. The outer liner is a special foam layer in the helmet's crown, made of polystyrene or polypropylene. This layer helps absorb shock energy not isolated by the outer shell.

Foam walls are becoming a mainstay at NASCAR tracks, offering great crash protection. In this shot, Kyle Petty's Dodge would be banged up a lot worse (and perhaps Kyle also) if he hit the concrete wall without the protective barrier.

The inner liner is a form-fitting layer of a fire-retardant material of nylon, or Nomex, made by DuPont Chemical. This material does not burn, melt or support combustion. Cheek pads and chin straps on the helmet are also fireproof. The face shield is made of the tough but pliable Lexan plastic, which is also used in the windshields of a Cup car.

The threat of a car fire has diminished over the years, but is still possible. A driver's gear includes fire-retardant material such as Proban or Nomex, which is woven into the material used to make the driving suit, gloves, socks and shoes. The suits are rated in protecting drivers from second-degree burns of a gasoline fire, with time ranges between three and 40 seconds.

The latest innovation in personal driver safety is the HANS (head and neck support) device. This apparatus was designed to reduce the chance of injury caused by unrestrained movement of a driver's head during a crash. Built of carbon fiber and Kevlar, the HANS device is a semi-hard collar held onto the upper body by a harness worn by the driver. Weighing 1.5 pounds, two flexible tethers attach the collar to the helmet, which helps hold the head from snapping forward or sideways.

Developed by engineering professor Dr. Robert Hubbard and sports car racer Jim Downing, the HANS device was initially accepted and proven in other forms of motor-sport, but not stock car racing. The deaths of NASCAR Cup drivers Adam Petty, Kenny Irwin, Tony Roper and Dale Earnhardt since May 2000 have changed this view. All four were killed when their cars slammed into a wall, and

the drivers suffered fractures to the base of the skull. In October 2001, NASCAR mandated a head and neck restraint for drivers in all of its classes.

Retaining walls

While there are Nextel Cup races at many different tracks, all tracks have one thing in common – concrete retaining walls. These walls contain a car to the racing area in the event of a crash or loss of control. However, the walls do not absorb any energy or have any give, making any contact with them possibly treacherous.

To rectify this potentially dangerous situation, energy-absorbing barriers of crushable material have been installed at some tracks, dissipating the force of the impact. Presently there are several types of these "soft walls" at racetracks.

A block of foam surrounded by polystyrene, known as Cellofoam, has been used at the Lowe's Motor Speedway in turns two and four with good results. Another soft wall system, championed by the Indy Racing League and used at Indianapolis Motor Speedway, is PEDS (polyethylene energy dissipating system). This involves small polyethylene cylinders installed inside larger ones, absorbing the impact of a crashing car.

IPS (impact protection system) is a soft wall design made of layered PVC material with an integrated honeycomb structure. The inner piece of this wall is then wrapped in a rubber casing. These walls are segmented and attached to the concrete walls with cables.

The newest proposal in this development at stock car speedways is the SAFER (steel and foam energy reduction) system. Developed by the University of Nebraska, this system is comprised of four steel tubes welded into 20-foot sections. It is then bolted to the wall with hard pink foam between it and the outer concrete wall. The SAFER system is currently installed on a 3,000-foot section in turn four of Talladega Speedway, and there are plans to have the entire racing perimeter set up.

Daytona International Speedway also has plans of installing the system around the track later in 2004. Talladega and Daytona will join five other tracks – Indianapolis, Richmond, New Hampshire, Phoenix and Homestead-Miami – with these protective barriers. NASCAR officials would like to have all tracks it races at set up with some type of energy-absorbing wall system by 2005.

The soft wall technology has not been fully accepted, as some flaws in the systems have been cited. If a wall of a breakable material is hit, then there is a time delay in cleaning up the pieces and replacing the damaged area.

Another criticism is that a car can bounce off a soft wall back into oncoming traffic – with disastrous results. Also, with Cup cars driving so close to the wall to get the best racing line when setting up for the turns, a car could scrape against the soft wall at such an angle that it could get caught in the material and lose control.

As a testament to the strong, heavily protected driver's compartment in today's NASCAR vehicle, Ryan Newman walked away from this after the car got airborne and rolled three times before stopping on its roof. Note the rear axle is missing from the Alltel Dodge. "I was just in the wrong place at the wrong time," said Newman after the 2003 Daytona 500 accident. "I'll tell you this, Disney World doesn't have anything like that."

Opposite: After some trepidation, HANS devices are now universal in NASCAR Cup racing. Here's Dale Earnhardt Jr. doing the modeling.

PIT STOPS

Colorful, vibrant and packed with action, pit stops have become a fan favorite and in some instances can be more exciting than the race itself.

Pit stops are an important and integral part of a race. What was once a leisurely activity for refueling and getting new tires has turned into a series of highly disciplined skills, where time and teamwork are of the essence. An event can be won or lost in a pit stop.

When a race car comes into the pits for service, what appears to be semi-organized chaos is actually a well-rehearsed routine like no other. Moving in compete harmony, seven team members jump over the pit wall with their tools and equipment to fuel the car, change tires and perform other on-the-spot duties such as suspension adjustments.

All this is performed in under 18 seconds, and then the race car is back on its way. Try to get 22 gallons of gas, four new tires and the windshield cleaned in that time at your local service station.

Jackman

This team member is the first and last person to touch the car when in the pits. The jackman is ready with a lightweight (35-pound) aluminum jack and has the car's right side up in the air almost before the car comes to a complete stop. A good jackman gets the car up with one-and-a-half pumps on the jack lever. He then stays with the car to make sure it remains stable during the tire changes, and keeps the loose tires out of the way. He also helps the rear tire changer in discarding the

used tires. When the right side is complete, he rushes to the driver's side, performs the same duties, and when all team members have completed their tasks, he lets the car down, which is the signal to the driver to exit the pits.

Gas man

The gas man is one of a two-person team, and his duty is to manually fill the race car's fuel cell with up to 22 gallons of fuel. Using two 11-gallon containers, the gas man rams the container's spring-loaded neck into the car's fuel cell plate, which is also spring-loaded. When these connect, a vacuum is created that allows for maximum fuel flow from the container into the fuel cell. This way there is no backflow – something that could happen when you're filling your average car at a service station, causing gas to spill all over your clothes and shoes.

Catch can man

This team member assists the gas man by holding the first 11-gallon container in place on the car while the gas man readies the second container. He also operates a flap on a one-inch pipe that leads to the fuel cell in the car. By opening this flap, air is forced out of the fuel cell so the maximum amount of fuel can be loaded. If there is any overflow, the excess fuel

will be pushed out of this small pipe and caught in a can. For obvious reasons, both the gas man and the catch can man wear fire-retardant clothing.

Tire changers

There are two tire changers on each team. One changes the front tires, and the other changes the rear tires. When a car is in the air, the changer quickly removes the tire using an air gun. The new tires and wheels have their five lug nuts stuck on the wheel beforehand to speed up fastening them to the car. Although the changers' tools are called air guns, they operate on nitrogen rather than compressed air. Nitrogen is used because compressed air contains moisture that could damage these guns.

Tire carriers

These two crew members carry the 60-pound front and rear tires and wheels to the race car, and also assist the tire changers. A carrier will help a changer in case there's a stuck wheel, and the front tire carrier will clean away any debris from the front of the car while the jackman is changing sides. The carriers always ensure that a discarded tire is laid flat on the pavement so it doesn't roll away into a moving race car or another team member.

Try to get 22 gallons of gas, four new tires and the windshield cleaned in 18 seconds at your service station.

THE BUSINESS OF NASCAR

The crowd at Bristol: A packed house.

Although organized stock car racing has been around for more than half a century, it has never been as popular as it is now. From their rural roots, NASCAR races have grown to two- and three-day events in most of the largest U.S. urban centers. NASCAR's top class, the Nextel Cup, is the No. 2 sport in North America, second only to major league football. Sales of licensed NASCAR merchandise is over $2 billion per year.

Tickets

In 2003, seven million fans bought tickets to its 36 races, with an average event attendance of 186,000. Ticket prices have skyrocketed since NASCAR's early days. In 1959, a spectator ticket in the Oldfield section of the Daytona International Speedway was $8. To sit in the same seat for the running of the 2003 Daytona 500 cost $120.

Television

NASCAR has television deals worth $2.8 billion with the FOX, NBC and TNT networks until 2008. In 1979, CBS paid Daytona International Speedway $1.5 million for broadcast rights. Now the FOX and NBC networks pay about $9 million for the running of the Daytona 500. A TV commercial during the 1979 Daytona broadcast cost between $25,000 and $30,000. The same air time now costs advertisers more than $150,000.

Sponsorship

Corporations spend an estimated $1 billion each year in sponsorships and promotions. New series sponsor Nextel Communications signed a 10-year agreement with NASCAR worth $750 million, which took effect January 1, 2004.

Cars have become rolling billboards. Of the more than 250 companies involved with NASCAR, 70 are Fortune 500 companies. The once-traditional automotive-related sponsorship has made room for household consumer products from Kellogg's, Coca-Cola, Pepsi, Kodak and Procter & Gamble.

A primary or main sponsorship with a Cup car team costs $3 million to $6 million per year. This usually gets the product name on the car's hood and quarter panels. A logo on the car's trunk lid – known as the "TV panel," as it can be seen from the following car's television camera – can cost up to $1 million for the season. At the other end of the scale, a 20-inch decal situated on the car's sides costs about $2,000 per race, but since it must be posted for each of the season's 36 races, this adds up to an annual cost of $72,000.

Top: Fans get up close and personal with their favorite driver, listening to the team chatter during a race.

Above: One of NASCAR's most expensive billboards. The "TV panel," shown here on Jimmie Johnson's Chevy, can fetch up to $1 million per season.

POINTS & SCORING

Matt Kenseth, 2003 Cup champ, sharing in the spoils of victory. Note the label on the bottle.

Starting in 2004, NASCAR officials modified the scoring system for the Nextel Cup. The previous system, which had been in place since 1975, was altered to add more excitement and to put an emphasis on winning races. Officials hope these modifications will generate more enthusiasm for the sport as the season progresses, as attendance and television ratings have traditionally dropped off in the fall.

In previous years, a team could claim the championship through consistency rather than winning more of the races. Matt Kenseth took the 2003 championship with only one victory, while Ryan Newman captured a series-high eight wins the same year but placed sixth.

In the new scoring system, after the first 26 races of the 36-race season, the teams in the top-10 in points standings – as well as any other teams within 400 points of the leader – will earn the right to take part in the "Chase for the Championship."

Drivers who qualify will have their points adjusted. The first-place team will begin the final 10 races with 5,050 points, the second team 5,045 points and so on, with incremental drops of five points for the remainder of the drivers.

Points

The points system in Nextel Cup competition may seem complicated at first, but it is a thor-

ough and fair system that also offers bonus points throughout the season.

Every one of the 36 Cup races is worth the same amount of points (except the special Bud Shootout and "The Winston," which do not qualify). There are no "unimportant" races on the schedule, so teams must perform their best at each race, whether it's the Daytona 500 or the Sharpie 500 at Bristol.

Bonus points are an important part of any race and can help a driver's standings.

- Any driver that leads any lap of a race gets five bonus points
- The driver that leads the most laps of the race gets five bonus points.

After each race, points are distributed as follows:

PLACE	POINTS	PLACE	POINTS	PLACE	POINTS	PLACE	POINTS
1st	180	12th	127	23rd	94	34th	61
2nd	170	13th	124	24th	91	35th	58
3rd	165	14th	121	25th	88	36th	55
4th	160	15th	118	26th	85	37th	52
5th	155	16th	115	27th	82	38th	49
6th	150	17th	112	28th	79	39th	46
7th	146	18th	109	29th	76	40th	43
8th	142	19th	106	30th	73	41st	40
9th	138	20th	103	31st	70	42nd	37
10th	134	21st	100	32nd	67	43rd	34
11th	130	22nd	97	33rd	64		

OFFICIALS

The race starter on the podium, as shown here at the 2004 Daytona 500, has the most important duties on race day. He is "the man" during an event.

Along with all the teams and thousands of fans at a Nextel Cup event, an important and necessary part of any race is the officiating staff.

A large team of dedicated men and women travel each week to each and every race to operate, score and officiate. There's more to running a race than just a person waving flags at the start/finish line. Dozens of officials register entrants, inspect the race cars to guarantee they meet rulebook standards, score each competitor during the race and ensure the track and its environs are absolutely first-rate for safe racing.

Here's a breakdown on some of the sanctioning body's duties.

Race control

This is the heart and nerve center of a race. Located in a tower with a good view of the track, all decisions are made here regarding all aspects of the race operation. It is here that officials "call" the race, telling the flag person and corner workers when the race starts, when there's an incident on the track requiring a caution period and any other instances in controlling the race.

An important part of race control is the scoring team. This group collects data on each race car once the race begins, and records each car's progress as the event progresses. Not only is this process recorded visually with video, there are four methods used to ensure the utmost in reliable, honest race information. NASCAR uses transponders, electronic buttons, manual (visual) scoring and automatic scoring.

Transponders are small devices, about the size of a pack of playing cards, which are affixed to each car in the race. These devices constantly transmit signals to the scorers, and the signals are decoded by computers.

Another scoring method involves the electronic button system. Each competing team provides a person who activates this counting system by pushing a button each time his or her team's car crosses the track's scoring line in the race. This may be repetitious, but is a necessity and involves a great deal of concentration.

Then there's the old tried-and-true method of physically tallying each lap of a car by hand on a lap chart, a method used since the dawn of auto racing, and which still has its place in today's computerized environment.

The final scoring method, which is used as a backup procedure only if necessary, is a computer-generated program which records the progress of each race car from flag to flag for the entire race.

Inspection

Technical inspection is an important aspect in stock car racing. Starting when the teams first roll into the track days before the actual race, inspectors armed with special tools and equipment check every piece of every car from engine specifications to tire sizes to body panel configuration. Through these inspections all cars race on an equal basis. Winning cars are also "torn down" (semi-dismantled) to ensure all parts are within regulations.

Pit road

Pit stops play an exciting and important role in stock car racing, and officials are constantly working on pit row, monitoring the pit stops and enforcing the rules that govern proper pit stop procedures.

The pit road officials also monitor to the control tower and respective team crew chiefs, noting any potential problems while the car is in the pits for servicing.

THE FLAG STAND

One of auto racing's most dominant visions is the flag waving. In NASCAR racing, an official starter is placed in a special stand directly above the track's start/finish line. The starter, through constant radio contact with race control, administers the running of the race through the use of a set of flags. Each flag has a specific purpose and is universal throughout all forms of motor sports.

 GREEN: Used at the beginning of a race, and at restarts. As with a green traffic light on city streets, this means the track is clear and racing may proceed.

 YELLOW: Denotes a caution period where the track is not clear as deemed by race officials. The yellow flag is displayed for an accident, track debris or unfavorable weather conditions. In most cases, cars must maintain their positions at the time this flag is displayed, and passing is not allowed. However, caution laps count as real laps.

RED: Signifies there is a situation on the racetrack which is unsafe, and cars must stop as quickly as possible. This flag may appear when an incident occurs that mandates the use of safety or repair crews, if the track is blocked or, in stock car racing, a heavy rain makes track conditions unsafe to continue.

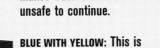 **BLUE WITH YELLOW:** This is an information flag, and it is waved at a driver who is about to be overtaken by a faster car. Usually the driver of the slower car will make room to be overtaken at the first available opportunity.

 BLACK: The black flag is displayed to an individual car due to a mechanical problem noted by officials or a rules infraction. A car must enter the pits when black-flagged.

 WHITE: Signifies there is one lap remaining in a race.

 BLACK WITH WHITE: Shown to a car that refuses to pit after several laps of black-flag racing. If the driver does not acknowledge this condition, officials cease to score for the car in question.

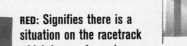 **YELLOW WITH RED:** Used on road courses, this flag is displayed by course workers at any given position on the course, signifying a track condition nearby that poses a potential hazard, such as oil on the track or a car blocking the course.

 CHECKERED: Waved at the end of the race when the scheduled distance has been completed.

TRACKS

Bristol's half-mile is one of the smallest and most popular NASCAR racing venues.

The 2004 Nextel Cup is comprised of 36 races at 23 different tracks in the United States. Far from the small dirt tracks and beach races of the past, today's races are held at state-of-the-art facilities ranging in track size from just over half a mile, like Martinsville and Bristol, to the over two-mile superspeedways of Daytona and Talladega.

While the majority of the races are run on oval-configuration tracks, there are two road-racing circuits on the schedule which highlight the Cup cars and drivers in a nontraditional setting.

The season kicks off on February 15 with the Daytona 500 – considered to be the greatest race on the schedule – and runs almost every Sunday thereafter to the season-ending Ford 400 at the Homestead-Miami Speedway November 21.

The majority of the tracks feature amenities such as private suites and boxes, upscale food concession stands and manufacturers' midways. Permanent fan seating ranges from 60,000 at North Carolina Speedway to 250,000 seats at the Indianapolis Motor Speedway for the Brickyard 400. All Nextel Cup races are broadcast live on television and radio.

ATLANTA MOTOR SPEEDWAY

Hampton, Ga.

TYPE: Oval

SIZE: 1.54 miles

BANKING IN CORNERS: 24°

DATE BUILT: 1959

FIRST CUP RACE: 1972

SEATING CAPACITY: 124,000

EVENTS: Golden Corral 500, Bass Pro Shops MBNA 500

CHICAGOLAND SPEEDWAY

Joliet, Ill.

TYPE: Tri-oval

SIZE: 1.5 miles

BANKING IN CORNERS: 18°

DATE BUILT: 2001

FIRST CUP RACE: 2001

SEATING CAPACITY: 75,000

EVENT: Tropicana 400

DOVER INTERNATIONAL SPEEDWAY

Dover, Del.

TYPE: Oval

SIZE: 1.0 miles

BANKING IN CORNERS: 24°

DATE BUILT: 1969

FIRST CUP RACE: 1972

SEATING CAPACITY: 140,000

EVENT: MBNA America 400

INFINEON RACEWAY

Sonoma, Calif.

TYPE: Road course

SIZE: 1.99 miles

BANKING IN CORNERS: varies

DATE BUILT: 1968

FIRST CUP RACE: 1989

SEATING CAPACITY: varies

EVENT: Dodge/Save Mart 350

BRISTOL MOTOR SPEEDWAY

Bristol, Tenn.

TYPE: Oval

SIZE: 0.533 miles

BANKING IN CORNERS: 36°

DATE BUILT: 1961

FIRST CUP RACE: 1972

SEATING CAPACITY: 160,000

EVENTS: Food City 500, Sharpie 500

DARLINGTON RACEWAY

Darlington, S.C.

TYPE: Oval

SIZE: 1.366 miles

BANKING IN CORNERS: 25°

DATE BUILT: 1949

FIRST CUP RACE: 1972

SEATING CAPACITY: 65,000

EVENTS: Carolina Dodge Dealers 400, Mountain Dew Southern 500

HOMESTEAD-MIAMI SPEEDWAY

Homestead, Fla.

TYPE: Oval

SIZE: 1.5 miles

BANKING IN CORNERS: 20°

DATE BUILT: 1995

FIRST CUP RACE: 1999

SEATING CAPACITY: 72,000

EVENT: Ford 400

KANSAS SPEEDWAY

Kansas City, Kan.

TYPE: Tri-oval

SIZE: 1.5 miles

BANKING IN CORNERS: 15°

DATE BUILT: 2001

FIRST CUP RACE: 2001

SEATING CAPACITY: 80,000

EVENT: Banquet 400 presented by ConAgra Foods

CALIFORNIA SPEEDWAY

Fontana, Calif.

TYPE: D-shaped oval

SIZE: 2 miles

BANKING IN CORNERS: 14°

DATE BUILT: 1997

FIRST CUP RACE: 1997

SEATING CAPACITY: 92,000

EVENTS: Auto Club 500, Pop Secret 500

DAYTONA INTERNATIONAL SPEEDWAY

Daytona Beach, Fla.

TYPE: Tri-oval

SIZE: 2.5 miles

BANKING IN CORNERS: 31°

DATE BUILT: 1959

FIRST CUP RACE: 1959

SEATING CAPACITY: 165,000

EVENTS: Daytona 500, Pepsi 400

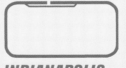

INDIANAPOLIS MOTOR SPEEDWAY

Speedway, Ind.

TYPE: Oval

SIZE: 2.5 miles

BANKING IN CORNERS: 9°

DATE BUILT: 1909

FIRST CUP RACE: 1994

SEATING CAPACITY: 250,000

EVENT: Brickyard 400

LAS VEGAS MOTOR SPEEDWAY

Las Vegas, Nev.

TYPE: Tri-oval

SIZE: 1.5 miles

BANKING IN CORNERS: 12°

DATE BUILT: 1995

FIRST CUP RACE: 1998

SEATING CAPACITY: 126,000

EVENT: UAW-DaimlerChrysler 400

LOWE'S MOTOR SPEEDWAY

Concord, N.C.

TYPE: Quad-oval

SIZE: 1.5 miles

BANKING IN CORNERS: 24°

DATE BUILT: 1959

FIRST CUP RACE: 1972

SEATING CAPACITY: 167,000

EVENTS: NASCAR Nextel All-Star Challenge, Coca-Cola 600, UAW-GM Quality 500

NEW HAMPSHIRE INTERNATIONAL SPEEDWAY

Loudon, N.H.

TYPE: Oval

SIZE: 1.058 miles

BANKING IN CORNERS: 18°

DATE BUILT: 1968

FIRST CUP RACE: 1972

SEATING CAPACITY: 91,000

EVENTS: New England 300, Sylvania 300

POCONO RACEWAY

Long Pond, Pa.

TYPE: Tri-oval

SIZE: 2.5 miles

BANKING IN CORNERS: 14°

DATE BUILT: 1968

FIRST CUP RACE: 1974

SEATING CAPACITY: 70,000

EVENTS: Pocono 500, Pennsylvania 500

TEXAS MOTOR SPEEDWAY

Fort Worth, Tex.

TYPE: Quad-oval

SIZE: 1.5 miles

BANKING IN CORNERS: 24°

DATE BUILT: 1997

FIRST CUP RACE: 1997

SEATING CAPACITY: 155,000

EVENT: Samsung/Radio Shack 500

MARTINSVILLE SPEEDWAY

Martinsville, Va.

TYPE: Oval

SIZE: 0.526 miles

BANKING IN CORNERS: 12°

DATE BUILT: 1947

FIRST CUP RACE: 1972

SEATING CAPACITY: 86,000

EVENTS: Advance Auto Parts 500, Subway 500

NORTH CAROLINA SPEEDWAY

Rockingham, N.C.

TYPE: Oval

SIZE: 1.017 miles

BANKING IN CORNERS: 25°

DATE BUILT: 1965

FIRST CUP RACE: 1972

SEATING CAPACITY: 60,000

EVENT: Subway 400

RICHMOND INTERNATIONAL RACEWAY

Richmond, Va.

TYPE: Oval

SIZE: 0.75 miles

BANKING IN CORNERS: 14°

DATE BUILT: 1946

FIRST CUP RACE: 1972

SEATING CAPACITY: 105,000

EVENTS: Chevy American Revolution 400, Chevy Rock and Roll 400

WATKINS GLEN INTERNATIONAL

Watkins Glen, N.Y.

TYPE: Road course

SIZE: 2.45 miles

BANKING IN CORNERS: varies

DATE BUILT: 1949

FIRST CUP RACE: 1986

SEATING CAPACITY: varies

EVENT: Sirius at the Glen

MICHIGAN INTERNATIONAL SPEEDWAY

Brooklyn, Mich.

TYPE: Tri-oval

SIZE: 2 miles

BANKING IN CORNERS: 18°

DATE BUILT: 1968

FIRST CUP RACE: 1972

SEATING CAPACITY: 82,000

EVENTS: Sirius 400, GFS Marketplace 400

PHOENIX INTERNATIONAL RACEWAY

Avondale, Ariz.

TYPE: Oval

SIZE: 1 mile

BANKING IN CORNERS: 11°

DATE BUILT: 1964

FIRST CUP RACE: 1988

SEATING CAPACITY: 100,000

EVENT: Checker Auto Parts 500

TALLADEGA SUPERSPEEDWAY

Talladega, Ala.

TYPE: Tri-oval

SIZE: 2.66 miles

BANKING IN CORNERS: 33°

DATE BUILT: 1969

FIRST CUP RACE: 1972

SEATING CAPACITY: 143,000

EVENTS: Aaron's 499, EA Sports 500

Opposite: Jeremy Mayfield leads a pack during the Auto Club 500 in May 2004 at Fontana in the California sunshine. A newer track, California Speedway opened in 1997.

TOP TEAMS

RICHARD CHILDRESS RACING

OWNER:
Richard Childress

CUP DRIVERS:
Kevin Harvick (No. 29),
Johnny Sauter (No. 30),
Robby Gordon (No. 31)

CREW CHIEFS:
Todd Berrier (Harvick),
Kevin Hamlin (Sauter),
Chris Andrews (Gordon)

FIRST SEASON: 1969

CAREER CUP WINS: 76

Kevin Harvick, the rising star of Richard Childress Racing (RCR), attributes his Nextel Cup success to what he's learned from his boss.

"Richard has been down every road there is to go, good and bad," said Harvick. "That experience has really helped me grow as a driver and a person."

One of the bad roads Richard Childress has been down is the reason Harvick's car is adorned with No. 29. In February 2001, Childress's best friend, Dale Earnhardt, was killed at Daytona. Four months later, the two legends would have celebrated the 20th anniversary of one of the most successful pairings in NASCAR history.

Childress had 285 Cup starts as a driver before turning the No. 3 car over to Earnhardt – for the first time in August of 1981 and for good in 1984. When Earnhardt was killed, he had won six of his seven Winston Cup championships for RCR and had helped propel the company into the sport's elite ranks. A week after Earnhardt's death, the car's famous number was switched to 29 and Harvick, who was also racing in the Busch Series, was put behind the wheel.

RCR was a one-car operation from 1969 until 1994, with the owner also driving, until Earnhardt raced 11 times in 1981. The team picked up No. 3 in 1976 and, even in retirement, it remains among racing's most evocative

symbols. With Earnhardt elsewhere for two years, Ricky Rudd drove the No. 3, picking up RCR's first pole in 1982 and first victory, at Riverside, in 1983.

Earnhardt returned in 1984, won two races and had a dozen top-five finishes, setting the tone for the next 17 years. Earnhardt took the Cup points title in 1986, repeated this in 1987 and had back-to-back championships again in 1990–91 and 1993–94. He was also-runner-up three times.

On the heels of that success, RCR began to expand in 1995, when NASCAR introduced the Craftsman Truck Series. RCR won the inaugural series title with Mike Skinner driving. Skinner moved up to Winston Cup when the team added a second full-time car in 1997.

In 2000, RCR folded its truck team but added two Busch Series entries. The next year, Harvick not only replaced Earnhardt in the Cup series and won rookie of the year, he also took the Busch points title, making Childress the first owner to win a championship in each of NASCAR's three divisions.

RCR expanded to three full-time Cup teams in 2002. The new car, No. 30, had three drivers in its first three years, but now has high hopes with the promising Johnny Sauter, who helped RCR to the 2003 Busch owner's championship. With Sauter joining Harvick and veteran Robby Gordon, RCR's future seems in good hands.

Opposite: Childress team driver Robbie Gordon (left) and team owner Richard Childress (right) celebrate a win at Infineon Raceway, June 2003.

Above: Kevin Harvick and Childress are all smiles after the Tropicana 400 win at Chicagoland, July 2002.

DALE EARNHARDT INC.

OWNER:
Teresa Earnhardt

CUP DRIVERS:
Dale Earnhardt Jr. (No. 8),
Michael Waltrip (No. 15)

CREW CHIEFS:
Tony Eury (Earnhardt Jr.),
Slugger Labbe (Waltrip)

FIRST SEASON: 1996

CAREER CUP WINS: 15

*Above: A NASCAR icon,
Dale Earnhardt at the
Napa Auto Parts 500
in Fontana, April 2000.*

It's not often that a garage becomes a tourist attraction, but not many garages bear the name of the legendary Dale Earnhardt.

Earnhardt, the fan favorite who died on the last lap of the 2001 Daytona 500, had an office in the three-bay garage in Mooresville, N.C., where he and his wife Teresa started Dale Earnhardt Incorporated (DEI) in the 1980s before fielding racing teams in 1996. DEI headquarters has now grown to 14 acres and 200,000 square feet of space, attracting a lot of out-of-town traffic, most of it featuring No. 3 or No. 8 flags, or both. Because of its massive size, DEI is often referred to as the "Garage Mahal."

Oddly enough, Earnhardt didn't drive for his own company. He was firmly entrenched at Richard Childress Racing. "But I've got to have something to do after my driving days are done, and something for these boys to go on," he once said.

When it came to stock car racing, Earnhardt neither pushed nor discouraged sons Kerry and Dale Jr. When both of them worked their way into the sport, it became the deciding factor for Dale and Teresa to establish the racing team.

DEI ran a limited schedule for its first three years, starting just 37 races with four different drivers. Then in 1999, Steve Park ran the company's first full Cup schedule. Dale Earnhardt Jr. also ran five races as a tune-up for his first Cup season the next year. In 2000, Park won one race, Earnhardt Jr. won a pair and DEI was on its way. The team has won at least three races every year since then.

Earnhardt took a gamble in 2001 when he moved to a three-entry Cup operation and hired his good friend Michael Waltrip to drive the No. 15 car. Waltrip, a well-traveled driver who had never won in 462 races, repaid Earnhardt's faith with a victory at the Daytona 500. Tragically, it was the same race in which the company's famous founder died.

If Waltrip was ever going to win a race, it was likely to be at Daytona or Talladega, because DEI had utterly conquered restrictor plate racing. As a driver, Earnhardt had uncanny success at Talladega, although he didn't win the Daytona 500 until his 20th try. His mastery of restrictor racing was passed on to DEI, and company technical leader Richie Gilmore was credited with crafting the perfect engines for

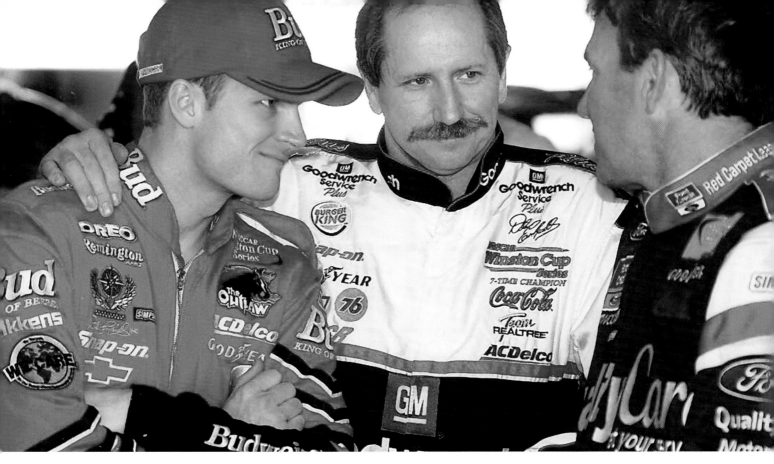

the superspeedways. Waltrip won the Daytona 500 again in 2003 and has also won at Talladega. The team won five straight races at Talladega until the streak was broken early in 2004.

"I think we work harder now than when we first started winning restrictor plate races," Gilmore said. "Because now people are looking at you as being the Chicago Bulls or New York Yankees of Talladega and Daytona. We take a lot of pride in that."

Earnhardt would have taken a lot of pride in the soaring career of his son. Earnhardt Jr. had two wins and 11 top-fives in 2002 and finished 11th in the points standings. He moved up to third overall in 2003 with another two wins.

Earnhardt Jr. opened 2004 with overwhelming dominance at Daytona, winning one of the Twin 125 Qualifiers early in the week, Sunday's emotional 500 and Monday's rain-delayed Busch Series race. That gave DEI 10 victories in the 13 most-recent restrictor plate races, including Dale Jr.'s three in the Busch Series in 2003.

"If you look back," said Earnhardt Jr., "it's a pretty surprising feat to have built the company into what we have today."

Three Dales. Dale Earnhardt Jr. (left) with Dad and Dale Jarrett at Daytona in 2000.

Left: Continuing the legacy, Dale Earnhardt Jr. helps celebrate his 2004 Daytona 500 win with step-mom Teresa Earnhardt.

EVERNHAM MOTORSPORTS

OWNER: Ray Evernham

CUP DRIVERS:
Kasey Kahne (No. 9),
Jeremy Mayfield (No. 19),
Bill Elliott (No. 91)

CREW CHIEFS:
Tommy Baldwin Jr.
(Kahne), Kenny Francis
(Mayfield), Sammy Johns
(Elliott)

FIRST SEASON: 2000

CAREER CUP WINS: 4

Above: Leaving as crew chief with the successful Jeff Gordon, Ray Evernham has done very well as a new team owner.

"I left probably the best job in motorsports and I took a lot of criticism for it."

After four tough years, Ray Evernham has put aside the negative comments and has put his Evernham Motorsports team in the forefront of NASCAR Nextel Cup competition. Many in the racing world questioned his move from crew chief of NASCAR superstar Jeff Gordon to forming his own Cup team, as well as running Dodges, cars unknown on the circuit after an absence of more than two decades.

Nevertheless, with more than 175 employees at a new shop in North Carolina, and a strong backing from the automaker, this former Modified driver from New Jersey has built the foundation for a winning team.

Starting in October 1999, Evernham began his partnership with Dodge, then signed veteran NASCAR driver Bill Elliott to the team the following March. The two Cup veterans captured the pole at the Daytona 500 in 2001, and the team won its first Cup victories at Pocono and Indianapolis that year. Evernham Motorsports was on the right track.

Known as "the crew chief of the 1990s,"

Evernham built a dynasty with Jeff Gordon and Hendrick Motorsports. Starting in 1992, this team won 45 Cup races and the Winston Cup championship three times. As successful as he was, however, Evernham wanted to leave and get out on his own.

"All along, we've been saying that we're building a good organization," Evernham said. "We're trying to do the right things. I feel good that some of the things we've put into place are working and I feel there is some chemistry in place."

Some of this "chemistry" has been the signing of rookie driver Kasey Kahne to the team, who has propelled himself to being one of the top drivers of 2004. Along with Kahne's success, Elliott captured a win at Rockingham in 2003, and with nine top-five and 12 top-10 finishes, placed ninth in the 2003 Cup standings. Other team driver Jeremy Mayfield placed 19th in the 2003 points race.

Evernham's commitment to detail and his building and implementation of modern pit crew methods has made him one of NASCAR's most respected leaders, and he has applied these characteristics to his team with outstanding success in such a short period of time.

Evernham's chemistry includes solid teamwork, shown here as the pit crew readies Jeremy Mayfield at Atlanta in March 2004.

Left: Evernham (center) and team celebrate their win at Indy, August 2002. That's Bill Elliott on the boss's left.

JOE GIBBS RACING

OWNER: Joe Gibbs

CUP DRIVERS:
Bobby Labonte (No. 18),
Tony Stewart (No. 20)

CREW CHIEFS: Michael
McSwain (Labonte),
Greg Zipadelli (Stewart)

FIRST SEASON: 1992

CAREER CUP WINS: 40

*Top: Bobby Labonte
and crew celebrate
after the victory at
Miami-Homestead,
November 2003.*

*Bottom: Joe Gibbs, a
winner in two sports.*

It's a gamble for Joe Gibbs to return to the dog-eat-dog world of pro football, but he also rolled the dice when he left the NFL for the equally competitive NASCAR.

Still, that move has turned out very well.

Gibbs won three Super Bowls during his 12-year tenure as Washington Redskins head coach. He came to NASCAR, starting in 1992, so he could spend more times with sons J. D. and Coy.

He first won stock car's biggest race when Dale Jarrett took the Daytona 500 in 1993. Joe Gibbs Racing won Cup points championships with Bobby Labonte in 2000, and again with Tony Stewart in 2002. Then in January 2004, Gibbs accepted an offer from the Redskins to return as head coach and president. J. D. Gibbs had already been president of Joe Gibbs Racing since 1997, so Joe decided to go back to football.

"It's a big learning curve," Gibbs said. "But I came into racing and we didn't know anything. I just had a love for it, and I learned on the job. Returning to football after more than a decade should be the same."

Gibbs began laying the groundwork for a Cup team in 1991 with business partner and fellow footballer Don Meredith, along with important input from Richard Petty and Hendrick Motorsports. They leased Hendrick engines and some shop space and hired Jarrett as their first driver. In the team's sophomore season, Jarrett won the Daytona 500 and finished fourth in points. Gibbs would later describe it as "one of my greatest thrills in sport."

By 1995, the team had a well-established shop near Charlotte, N.C., announced plans for an in-house engine program and signed Labonte as a driver. He won three races and the team's first pole that year. Switching to Pontiac from Chevy in 1997, Joe Gibbs Racing also heavily pursued open-wheel star Stewart, signing him to limited Busch Series appearances in 1997 and 1998 to prepare him for Cup racing. The careful planning paid off as Stewart won the outside pole at the 1999 Daytona 500, was fourth in the drivers' standings and was named Cup rookie of the year. Labonte won a career-high five races that year and finished second in points.

In 2000, Stewart won six times and Labonte won the points title. In 2002, Stewart gave the team its second points title in three years. Then in 2003, Jimmy Makar, Gibbs' crew chief since day one, moved up to vice-president of racing, and Michael "Fatback" McSwain came over from Robert Yates Racing and is now Labonte's crew chief. With its top drivers signed to long-term deals (Labonte to 2008 and Stewart to 2009), Joe Gibbs Racing is in good shape, even with the owner moving from track side to side-lines.

Hold your breath time. Tony Stewart's crew waits out the final laps of the MBNA 500 at Atlanta 2002. Stewart's win was his sixth for the team.

HENDRICK MOTORSPORTS

OWNER: Rick Hendrick

CUP DRIVERS:
Jeff Gordon (No. 24),
Jimmie Johnson (No. 48),
Terry Labonte (No. 5),
Brian Vickers (No. 25)

CREW CHIEFS:
Robbie Loomis (Gordon),
Chad Knaus (Johnson),
Jim Long (Labonte),
Peter Sospenzo (Vickers)

FIRST SEASON: 1985

CAREER CUP WINS: 117

Top: Pushing the Jeff Gordon Chevy after a win at Fontana in 2004.

Hendrick Motorsports has grown in perfect lock-step with the explosion of stock car racing.

As NASCAR has become more successful, so has Hendrick Motorsports (HMS). In its first 20 years of Cup racing, the company has won at least one pole every season, and at least one Cup race in 18 of those seasons. It is the only organization to have won four straight Cup championships (Jeff Gordon in 1995, 1997 and 1998, and Terry Labonte in 1996). When driver Brian Vickers won the Busch Series points title in 2003, it gave HMS victories in all three of NASCAR's national divisions: five at the Cup level, three (by Jack Sprague) in Craftsman Truck and one in Busch. Heading into 2004, HMS had 1,780 entries, with 32 drivers in 725 races, and had won 127 events on 24 different tracks.

Team owner Rick Hendrick bucked NASCAR tradition and started a new trend in 1993 when he gave a full-time ride to then-21-year-old Gordon, a rising open-wheel driver who was untested in stock cars. At the time, he didn't have a car or a sponsor for Gordon, but like so many other Hendrick innovations, the move

worked out spectacularly.

Still, it didn't start out quite so successfully. A former drag racer, who at 14 co-built his first machine with his legendary Modified-racing father, "Papa Joe," Rick Hendrick hoped to enter NASCAR as a co-owner with country singer Kenny Rogers in 1983, and with Richard Petty at the wheel. Then the deal fell apart, and he watched his first Daytona 500 from the roof of a motor home on the infield. He entered the Cup series as a solo effort with All-Star Racing in 1984, and Geoff Bodine driving. On the first qualifying lap at the Daytona 500, Hendrick didn't have a sponsor and then the engine blew out.

"All I wanted that first year was to make the race, and hoped that I didn't lose everything I had, trying to make it work," Hendrick recalled. "I'd be the biggest liar in the world if I said I was thinking I could win a championship some day."

Nevertheless, he did. Bodine took three races that first year, and by 1986, Hendrick broke with another tradition and fully committed to the multi-car team concept, bringing in talented Tim Richmond and later three-time

Cup champion Darrell Waltrip. He's kept adding winning drivers since then. Ricky Rudd, Ken Schrader, Todd Bodine, Ricky Craven, Jerry Nadeau, Joe Nemechek and even Al Unser Jr. have all raced for Hendrick.

At the same time that he was growing the racing team, Hendrick was creating one of America's largest automotive retail businesses, with more than 60 dealerships coast-to-coast. HMS's complex in Charlotte, which also builds the team's engines, has more than 400 employees. The company moved to four full Cup teams in 2002, and also entered the Busch Series on a full-time basis that year. Hendrick's son Ricky drove the Busch car, but has since moved up to co-owner of that car (with "Papa Joe"). Vickers won the Busch title in 2003 before moving up to the team's No. 25 car for the 2004 season.

In 1996, Rick Hendrick was diagnosed with leukemia, but in late 1999, the disease was declared in full remission. Hendrick has since become a national spokesman for bone marrow donations.

Above: A winning combination. Crew chief Robbie Loomis (left), team owner Rick Hendrick and driver Jeff Gordon celebrate the October 2003 Martinsville win.

PENSKE RACING

OWNER: Roger Penske

CUP DRIVERS:
Ryan Newman (No. 12),
Rusty Wallace (No. 2),
Brendan Gaughan (No. 77)

CREW CHIEFS:
Matt Borland (Newman),
Larry Carter (Wallace),
Shane Wilson (Gaughan)

FIRST SEASON: 1972

CAREER CUP WINS: 53

The Penske NASCAR team is just part of one of the most successful sports dynasties in the world. Former road racer Roger Penske has built a highly successful transportation company which includes vehicle leasing, as well as automotive retail and tire sales.

Penske Racing Inc. is the most successful Indy car team in history with 110 wins, including 11 Indy 500 victories.

In 1991, Penske returned to NASCAR cup racing with driver Rusty Wallace and sponsor Miller Brewing Company. Under the team name Penske Racing South Inc., Wallace heads up the present car team, which after nine seasons of driving Fords now runs Dodges. The other team drivers are Ryan Newman and Rookie Brendan Gaughan.

This collective is one of the most well-rounded teams in NASCAR in terms of driving ability. Veteran Wallace has 54 Cup victories to

his credit and is still a strong contender. He can also provide his advice and expertise to other team members. Wallace placed 14th in the 2003 Cup standings in his Miller Lite Dodge.

Ryan Newman has been a standout for the team. The Raybestos Rookie of the Year in 2002, Newman won eight Cup races in 2003 in the ALLTEL Dodge and placed sixth in the standings.

As with many NASCAR teams, Penske Racing South is headquartered in North Carolina. Some of its success must be credited to crew chiefs Larry Carter, who helped get Wallace back in victory lane in 2004, and former Penske CART member Matt Borland, who joined the Newman team as crew chief in 2002. New to the team is Brendan Gaughan. A former NASCAR Craftsman Truck Series competitor, he won six events in that series in 2003 and placed fourth in the standings.

Above: Ryan Newman and crew at Lowe's Motor Speedway May 2004 – just part of the Penske empire.

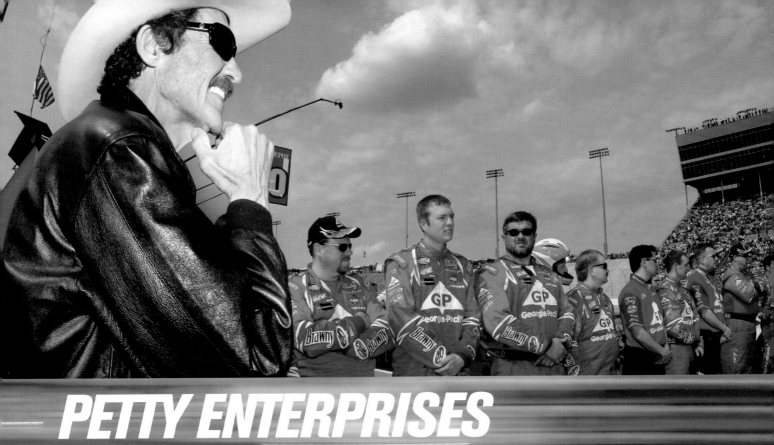

PETTY ENTERPRISES

The most famous name in stock car racing has always built and maintained its NASCAR cars since family patriarch Lee Petty started Petty Racing in 1949. Since that time, this team has produced four generations of drivers, something unheard of in professional sports.

Through hard work, perseverance and the help of Chrysler, the Petty name became a household word as Richard Petty drove a series of now-famous No. 43 Plymouths to many all-time NASCAR records in a career that debuted in 1958 and ended in 1992.

By 1979, third-generation family member Kyle Petty, Richard's son, started in NASCAR Cup racing from the Petty Enterprises shop at Level Cross, N.C. Maurice Petty, Richard's brother and the team's early engine builder, passed the wrenches to his son Tim in 1982, and this younger Petty began to build power plants as the team switched over to Pontiacs.

In 2000, the team suffered a double blow. Lee Petty died from surgery complications, and Kyle's son Adam was killed in a crash at a Busch practice session at New Hampshire International Speedway.

Despite these hardships, the team continued, and in 2001 renewed its association with Dodge. The next year legendary crew chief Robin Pemberton joined Petty and the team ended its in-house engine program, partnering with Mike Ege Racing Engines.

For 2003, the team fielded three cars. Kyle Petty ran 33 races and placed 37th. Former Busch Series and Craftsman Truck Series driver Jeff Green joined the Petty team, finishing 34th with 31 races in 2003.

The third Petty driver has a name just as famous as his team owners in racing circles: Christian Fittipaldi, who has competed in CART and Formula 1 racing, and is the nephew of former F1 champion Emerson Fittipaldi. After a limited Cup schedule in 2003 with 15 races, Fittipaldi placed 44th.

OWNERS: Richard and Kyle Petty

CUP DRIVERS:
Kyle Petty (No. 45),
Jeff Green (No. 43)

CREW CHIEFS:
Greg Steadman (Petty),
Gary Putnam (Green)

FIRST SEASON: 1949

CAREER CUP WINS: 268

Above: The King at Atlanta in March 2004. Richard Petty is still very active in racing.

ROUSH RACING

OWNER: Jack Roush

CUP DRIVERS:
Mark Martin (No. 6),
Jeff Burton (No. 99),
Kurt Busch (No. 97),
Greg Biffle (No. 16),
Matt Kenseth (No. 17)

CREW CHIEFS:
Pat Tryson (Martin),
Paul Andrews (Burton),
Jimmy Fennig (Busch),
Doug Richert (Biffle),
Robbie Reiser (Kenseth)

FIRST SEASON: 1988

CAREER CUP WINS: 66

Jack Roush has enjoyed so much success in the racing business it's difficult to believe that he didn't win a Cup points championship until 2003.

When Matt Kenseth captured that Winston Cup title, it completed a four-year binge in which Roush Racing became just the third organization to win all three of NASCAR's national series. Greg Biffle won the Craftsman Truck Series championship in 2000 and took Busch Series honors two years later.

One of the busiest owners in the racing business, Roush entered NASCAR in 1988 after two decades in drag racing and sports car racing. The driver he hired to get him started in stock cars, Mark Martin, is still with him. So are four other top drivers – Kenseth, Biffle, Jeff Burton and Kurt Busch – as Roush Racing fields the most cars in the Nextel Cup Series. The company also maintains a strong commitment to the Craftsman and Busch Series.

Jack Roush has always loved cars and speed – and combining the two. He has a master's degree in scientific mathematics from Eastern Michigan University, which he earned while working on processing car assembly at Ford

Motor Company. He left Ford in 1969 to start "The Fastbacks" – a group dedicated to designing and running drag racers. The group broke up within two years and Roush went to work as an engineer at Chrysler Corporation before forming another drag racing partnership with Wayne Gapp. Over the next few years, they won national titles in the National Hot Rod Association, the International Hot Rod Association and the American Hot Rod Association.

Roush was also providing engines for power boats and oval-track cars, and in 1978 he formed Jack Roush Performance Engineering to build engines for other teams. He gravitated toward sports cars in 1984, and over the next 14 years won 24 titles in the Sports Car Club of America and the International Motor Sports Association.

Martin gave Roush his first win, at Rockingham, in late 1989, a year after the team joined Cup racing. Over the next 14 years, Martin would finish third in the points race four times and second twice, losing the 1990 title to Dale Earnhardt by 26 points when he was penalized 46 points for an unintentional spacer infraction. Roush also got third-place finishes out of

Burton in 2000 and Busch in 2002, and had four drivers in the top-12 in 2002, but it took until the team's 16th full season before Kenseth won the points title.

"It's just large, I'm kind of in awe," said Roush after Kenseth ran away with the 2003 crown. "This is the kind of year I envisioned when we started this 15 years ago."

Roush's three companies – Roush Racing, Roush Performance and Roush Industries – employ more than 1,800 people and operate out of over 50 facilities in four different countries.

The man in the trademark straw hat almost wasn't around to enjoy any of it. In April 2002, Roush crashed his plane into a small lake in southern Alabama and was unconscious, submerged and strapped into the pilot's seat. Fortunately, a retired Marine saw the accident, dove into the water, found Roush and hauled him to the surface and resuscitated him. Despite multiple injuries, within six weeks Roush was back on the track – and winning races.

No, they're not flyers advertising next week's race, but checklists on Mark Martin's Ford. The work never stops.

Opposite top: With his team cheering him on, Roush driver Matt Kenseth celebrates his win at Rockingham in 2002.

Opposite bottom: Jack Roush entered the NASCAR arena after 20 years of drag, sports and oval car racing.

WOOD BROTHERS RACING

OWNER: Glen, Len and Eddie Wood, and Kim Wood Hall

CUP DRIVER: Ricky Rudd (No. 21)

CREW CHIEF: Ben Leslie (Rudd)

FIRST SEASON: 1953

CAREER CUP WINS: 96

Above: As part of NASCAR's oldest team, these Wood Brothers crew members carry on with the tradition, shown at Lowe's Motor Speedway in 2003.

Now in its 54th year of operation, the Wood Brothers Racing team goes back to the very beginnings of NASCAR.

Brothers Glen and Leonard Wood formed a team in 1950 to go racing in NASCAR's Modified ranks. What the Virginia brothers discovered was auto racing was serious business, even at that time. With Glen doing the driving, the team won several Sportsman and Modified titles in the 1950s, and placed third in NASCAR's Convertible division in 1957.

They continued racing until 1961, with four Grand National (now Nextel Cup) races to their credit. Glen Wood hung up his racing helmet to assume crew chief duties with his brother assisting, and they developed a winning pit strategy for drivers such as Cale Yarborough, Tiny Lund and Fireball Roberts during the 1960s.

Leonard is known as the forefather of the organized pit stop, and the team's efforts have been very successful through six decades. Aside from NASCAR competition, the Wood Brothers are credited with helping Jimmy Clark with the 1965 Indy 500, and they have close to 100 NASCAR victories. Perhaps their greatest success came during their association with driver David Pearson, winning Cup races 11 times in 1973 and 10 times in 1976.

Still highly active in NASCAR racing as a team owner, the Wood Brothers are the most successful team in Ford racing history with 97 victories, including 12 Daytona 500 wins. They still head up this family-operated enterprise in a new facility situated in Mooresville, N.C, and second-generation family members continue the work Glen and Leonard started.

Eddie Wood is the owner/team manager of the No. 21 Ford, along with team owner/engine builder Len Wood, driven this season by veteran Ricky Rudd. The team also employs the talent of crew chief Ben Leslie, a Michigan native who has worked on the crews of Kurt Busch and Mark Martin.

ROBERT YATES RACING

In 15 years, the NASCAR team of Robert Yates has built a strong record.
Since starting in 1989, the Yates team has produced 54 Cup wins, 40 pole positions and one Cup championship.

The 60-year-old Yates has a strong resume in engine building. He started drag racing in the late 1950s, but got out from behind the seat, and in 1968, this North Carolina native joined the successful Holman-Moody team. Yates then went to work for Junior Johnson and was in charge of that team's engine program, producing a lot of winners, including Bobby Allison, Darrell Waltrip and Cale Yarborough.

After several years of engine building, Yates decided to strike out on his own, forming a Cup team in 1989. With driver Davey Allison, the team was quite successful with 14 wins until Allison's death in 1993.

Yates then employed drivers Ernie Irvan, Robby Gordon and Kenny Wallace with limited success, but the effort really took hold with noted second-generation driver Dale Jarrett coming to drive for the team. With Jarrett at the wheel of the No. 88 Ford, the team was a strong contender for the next five years, winning the Cup championship in 1999.

Running a two-car team, Jarrett and Ricky Rudd drove Yates' cars to 11 wins, 71 top-five and 114 top-10 finishes between 2000 and 2002. It was also at this time the team acquired the sponsorship of United Parcel Service, and the brown UPS Ford is one of the most well-known sights in racing.

In 2003, Yates brought Elliott Sadler on board to complement Jarrett, and he placed 22nd in the final standings while Jarrett did not have a good season, finishing 27th in points.

Although 2003 was not the team's best season, Yates has regrouped with team members such as head engine builder Doug Yates and new crew chief Mike Ford. The team is adopting new technology in its quest for returning to the winner's circle and plans to make the most of this opportunity.

"You want to win, so you work hard," Yates said at the beginning of the 2004 season. "You've got to be smart enough, but a lot of it is about having opportunity. We have the opportunity, now we just have to capitalize on it in 2004."

OWNER: Robert Yates
CUP DRIVERS:
Elliott Sadler (No. 38),
Dale Jarrett (No. 88)
CREW CHIEFS:
Todd Parrott (Sadler),
Mike Ford (Jarrett)
FIRST SEASON: 1988
CAREER CUP WINS: 54

Above: Elliott Sadler and crew celebrate the 2004 Gatorade 125 win at Daytona.

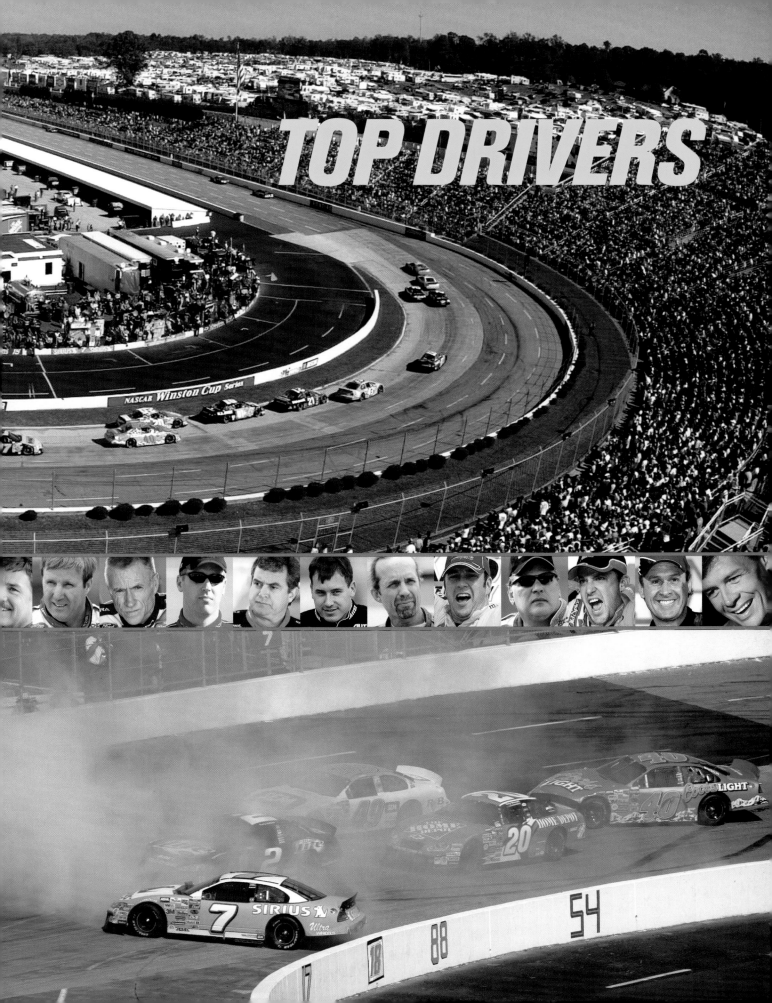

TOP DRIVERS

JEFF BURTON

NO. 99

BORN: June 29, 1967, South Boston, Va.

HOBBIES: Golf, boating

TEAM: Roush Racing

CAR: Ford

SPONSOR: Roush Racing

CUP WINS: 17

2003 CUP EARNINGS: $4,384,752

CAREER EARNINGS: $31,588,107

Jeff Burton has one of the thickest resumes of current stock car drivers, but at the start of the 2004 season racing fans were mostly talking about what was missing from it.

After winning 17 Cup races in five years, Burton entered the season in a 76-start winless slump and – worse – without a major sponsor. That led track-siders to speculate that Burton would jump teams from Roush Racing to Richard Childress Racing. However, owner Jack Roush guaranteed that Burton's No. 99 car would carry some partial sponsorship packages and race a complete season, even if the company had to pay out-of-pocket to do so.

"That (interest from other teams) has been flattering, but my allegiance is with Roush Racing," Burton said. "When things have been good, we've done them together, and when things have gone bad, we've gone through them together."

The team has had to go through difficult times more often than good in the new millennium. After four straight seasons in the top five in points standings, Burton dropped to 10th in 2001, and 12th in each of the next two years. A new over-the-wall crew was formed in 2003, and after a stuttering start to the 2004 season, Bob Osborne came in as the new crew chief to try to turn things around. Then there was the sponsorship problem – a reflection of the spiraling costs of financing a NASCAR team.

"It's an agonizing sport when things go wrong," said Burton. It's deeply gratifying when they go right, though, and for most of his exemplary racing career, much has gone right for Burton.

He grew up watching his older brother Ward race go-karts in their hometown of South Boston, Va., and when he was 7 years old, Jeff climbed behind a steering wheel himself. Eventually, he won two state titles and was the runner-up four times before graduating to pure stocks in 1984, the year he turned 17.

In his second full season, Burton won six Late Model races. Then in 1988, he won seven of the 21 Late Model features at South Boston Speedway and was voted the track's most popular

driver. That same season he entered five NASCAR Busch Series races, driving a car owned by his father, John. In 1989, he had two top-fives and six top-10s, and the next year captured his first Busch win at Martinsville. He followed that up with 12th-place finishes in the 1991 and 1992 points standings.

Burton made his Cup debut in 1993 at New Hampshire International Speedway, finishing 37th after qualifying sixth. It was his only Cup race of the season, but it was enough to attract the attention of Stavola Brothers Racing, and they signed him for 1994. He responded with two top-fives, three top-10s and the rookie of the year award, beating his older brother Ward.

After another year with the Stavolas, where

Burton inches ahead of Rusty Wallace at Michigan in 2003. Burton placed 11th.

"It's an agonizing sport when things go wrong."

his best finish was fifth, Burton moved to Roush Racing in 1996 and finished in the top-five six times, jumping all the way to 13th in the points standings from 32nd the year before.

In 1997, he took the checkered flag early in the season at the Texas 500 for his first Cup victory, which was also the inaugural premier series race for the Texas Motor Speedway. He won again at New Hampshire and Martinsville, added 10 more top-fives and announced that he had arrived for good with his fourth-place finish in the drivers' standings. He would spend four straight years among the elite five.

Burton was fifth in 1998, winning twice and establishing a career-high with 18 top-five finishes, a total he matched the following season. But in 1999, he also led all drivers with six wins, including rain-shortened victories at both Darlington races.

He tied for the most victories in 2000, with four, and finished third in the points race behind Bobby Labonte and Dale Earnhardt. His Ford ran so well he had only two DNFs – fewer than all but three drivers in the premier series. In Burton's victories that year at Las Vegas and Darlington, his brother Ward was the runner-up.

With the entire sport in turmoil after Dale Earnhardt's death at the 2001 Daytona 500, Burton, always an advocate for enhanced safety measures, became an unofficial spokesperson for improved protection for drivers.

"This is an expedition," he said. "We are a group who have watched people trying to climb Mt. Everest. We watched some succeed and some do not so well. But now we're at the base of the mountain and we're creating a plan to get to the top of it, faster, safer and better than anyone else has ever done."

Burton won twice in that 2001 season, but heading into his victory at the Coca-Cola 600 he was mired at 25th on the points ladder. He ended up 10th overall. "People kept saying that this would be when we turned it around, but we never quite did," he said.

It didn't turn around in 2002 or 2003 either, when he didn't win and totaled only eight top-five finishes. But he is determined to overcome both his victory and sponsorship droughts.

"When I see a No. 99 decal on somebody's pickup truck, that means something to me," he said. "That's my number and I have unfinished business."

KURT BUSCH

There's a lot to be said for being a "Young Gun," as long as you know when to keep it in the holster, and as long as your aim is straight.

Kurt Busch, a central figure in NASCAR's expanding arsenal of Young Guns, admits he's had some problems adjusting to his mercurial rise to the sport's upper ranks. Lacking extended experience, his ability to handle emotional situations didn't develop as quickly as his driving skills. On the track, he has sometimes crossed the line between aggressiveness and belligerence.

That concept was crystallized in August 2003 when, after the Michigan 400, Jimmy Spencer reached into the cockpit of the Rubbermaid No. 97 Ford and punched Busch. It was the culmination of the two drivers' running feud and came after Spencer and several others thought Busch had tried to run Spencer into a fence. Both drivers were put on probation; Spencer was suspended for a week and fined $25,000 and Busch was fined $10,000 for what NASCAR called "unprofessional" behavior.

Busch later apologized to racing fans, to Roush Racing and to his sponsors, and he promised to be "less colorful" in the future. "But I know words are cheap and my commitment will be judged by what I do in the months ahead," he said.

There has never been any doubt about Busch's commitment to driving, nor his ability

NO. 97

BORN: August 4, 1978, Las Vegas, Nev.

HOBBIES: Jet skiing, water skiing

TEAM: Roush Racing

CAR: Ford

SPONSOR: Sharpie

CUP WINS: 8

2003 CUP EARNINGS: $5,587,384

CAREER EARNINGS: $13,183,351

to do so. He is so talented that in 2001 owner Jack Roush decided not to apprentice him in the Busch Grand National ranks and brought him right from the Craftsman Truck Series into what was then the Winston Cup circuit at the tender age of 22. Roush cited Busch's adaptability and skill at reading new tracks, but critics felt the rapid rise also deprived the young star of learning how to handle himself.

Busch has always been a quick learner. He grew up in Las Vegas, the son of parents who had moved to Nevada from a Chicago suburb. His father, Tom, was an auto mechanic, a tool salesman and a dominant driver on Las Vegas short tracks. Starting at age 8, Busch would run home from school to work in his father's

garage. His brother Kyle, seven years younger, would later follow suit.

"My father was so successful, nobody liked him at all," Busch once said. " I think he lost three races in three years, or something like that. There is only one way to see it. My dad is responsible for me racing and being where I am today. He always gave me a lesson to learn, then bent over backwards to help me."

Busch began his career racing go-karts, but it was in Dwarf cars where he made his first impression, winning the 1994 rookie of the year in Nevada at the age of 16 and the championship the next season. By 1996, he was Hobby Stock Champion at Las Vegas Speedway Park. In 1998, he was named rookie of the year in

NASCAR's Southwest Touring series, and he won the touring title the next season. That same year, an audition with Roush got him a spot in the NASCAR Craftsman Truck Series.

In 2000, he won four events and finished second in the Craftsman Truck points series, which prompted Roush to bring him directly to the sport's biggest stage for the 2001 season. He was runner-up to Kevin Harvick for rookie of the year and was 27th in points, with three top-fives. He was regarded as a nice young man.

Then Roush made an inspirational move, shifting veteran crew chief Jim Fennig from Mark Martin's to Busch's car, and sending Ben Leslie, Busch's crew chief, over to Martin. By March, Busch had won his first Winston Cup race (at Bristol) and followed up with one third-place and three second-place finishes. He had a string of poor finishes in August, so no one was really prepared for how the 2002 season ended: Busch won three of the last five events on the schedule, including back-to-back victories at Martinsville and Atlanta, and was third and sixth in the other two races.

"Getting my first Winston Cup victory is something I will never forget, but finishing the season like we did was just unreal," said Busch, who credited Fennig for the breakthrough season, where he placed third in the points race.

Buoyed by the 2002 finish, Busch started 2003 with a burst, winning once and finishing second twice in the first six races. But between April and October, his car suffered blown engines, blown tires and other problems, and his Sharpie team had numerous finishes outside the top-10. He won four races again, but could do no better than 11th in the points standings. Then, of course, there was the infamous incident with Spencer.

Busch also won the IROC four-race series, including a checkered flag at Talladega. His loss by inches to Ricky Craven at the Darlington Spring Race was considered by many to be the "finish" of the 2003 season.

"We put ourselves in a position to win a lot and built on our success," he told reporters. "We just had a lot of DNFs with motor troubles and being at the wrong place at the wrong time on the tracks.

"I know how quick this sport can beat you down. It challenges you in so many ways."

Busch in the pits at Atlanta Motor Speedway, October 2003.

"I know words are cheap and my commitment will be judged by what I do in the months ahead."

DALE EARNHARDT JR.

NO. 8

BORN: October 10, 1974, Kannapolis, N.C.

HOBBIES: Car restoration, computers

TEAM: Dale Earnhardt Inc.

CAR: Chevrolet

SPONSOR: Budweiser

CUP WINS: 10

2003 CUP EARNINGS: $6,880,807

CAREER EARNINGS: $20,642,359

Stock car racing may never see another moment like it.

As Dale Earnhardt Jr. roared across the 2004 Daytona 500 finish line ahead of friend Tony Stewart, some 200,000 rabid fans – every one of them on their feet – cried and roared their approval as if they had won the race themselves.

In a way they had. There wasn't a person anywhere in the racing world who didn't understand the emotional significance of that checkered flag. Earnhardt Jr. won the most prestigious of all stock car races in just his fifth attempt, just three years and 500 yards removed from where his famous had been killed, and six years to the day after the legendary No. 3 had

won his first Daytona 500 on his 20th try.

With the victory, the son emerged from the massive shadow cast by his father, but there will never be any true separation of the two Dale Earnhardts. They are forever linked by blood, by success and by the Daytona 500.

"My dad was in the passenger seat, having a blast," Earnhardt Jr. said through tears after the win. "Every time we come to Daytona we all feel it. In a way, it feels like you're closer to Dad. But at the same time, it's a reminder of losing him all over again.

"This is the greatest day of my life. You can't really describe it. I don't know if I'll ever be able to tell this story to anybody and really get it right."

When Earnhardt Jr. won the Busch Series race the next day, it completed a dominant Daytona unlike any before it. He won one of the Gatorade 125 qualifying races, the 500 itself and the Busch race, giving him nine career victories at Daytona.

Earnhardt Jr. and his father joined the ranks of Lee and Richard Petty, and Bobby and Davey Allison as the only father/son winners of the prestigious 500.

Like most sons of top drivers, Earnhardt Jr. was born to race.

His grandfather Ralph won the 1956 NASCAR Sportsman Division title, and Dale Jr. grew up watching his father win race after race, and a record-tying seven premier Cup series

championships. He also watched his father come so close but keep coming up short in the Daytona 500, and says that's when a desire to win the sport's biggest race began to take form.

"Little E" began his professional career at the age of 17 in the street stock division at Concord Motorsport Park in 1992, and later moved up to the Late Model stocks. His first car was a 1978 Monte Carlo he and brother Kerry bought for $500. In those days he raced against both Kerry and their sister Kelley.

From 1994 to 1996, Earnhardt Jr. won three NASCAR Late Model feature races, then made his Busch Series debut in 1996, finishing 14th at Myrtle Beach. He competed a limited schedule on NASCAR's second-best circuit until he went

Earnhardt Jr. does the victory dance after winning the Chevy American Revolution 400 at Richmond, his third win of 2004.

"My dad was in the passenger seat, having a blast."

full-time in 1998, when he won seven races, three poles and the points championship. He won the series title again in 1999, and also made five appearances on the premier circuit, with a 10th place finish at Richmond.

When team Dale Earnhardt Inc. (DEI) decided Earnhardt Jr. was ready for full-time duty in NASCAR's premier series, Budweiser came aboard with a massive five-year sponsorship deal. In 2000, he finished 16th in Cup Series points, losing the rookie of the year by 42 points to Busch Series rival Matt Kenseth. He took his first checkered flag at Texas Motor Speedway, and also won at Richmond, matching Davey Allison's 1987 record with two wins in his first 16 Cup appearances. He was also the first rookie to win the Winston all-star race.

Then came the tragedy of 2001, when Dale Earnhardt Sr. was killed on the last corner of the final lap at Daytona, the season's opening race. Michael Waltrip of DEI won the race, the first of his career, and Dale Jr. finished second.

Four days after burying his father, Earnhardt Jr. raced at Rockingham, but he hit a wall and didn't finish a lap. Five months later at Daytona, Earnhardt Jr. held off Waltrip to win the Pepsi 400 on the track that had brought him so much fortune and pain.

"That was one of the coolest moments in racing," Kenseth said at the time. "I was happier

for him than if I had won."

Earnhardt Jr. finished eighth in series points that year, winning twice more, including at Talladega, where his father's victory the year before was the last of his career. In 2002, his two wins came at Talladega, and he finished 11th in points, leading more laps than any other driver. He won Talladega again in 2003, his record fourth straight win at the superspeedway, and went from 38th to runner-up in the season's second race there. He also won all three races he entered in the Busch Series as owner/driver for Chance 2 Motorsports. His third-place finish in the 2003 Cup Series was his best ever and foreshadowed his brilliant start to the next season.

Although he had nine career victories entering the 2004 season, none could compare to that Pepsi 400 in Daytona.

"That was the most emotional win ever," he said then.

He didn't know what was coming.

BILL ELLIOTT

NO. 9

BORN: October 5, 1955, Dawsonville, Ga.

HOBBIES: Flying, skiing

TEAM: Evernham Motorsports

CAR: Dodge

SPONSOR: Evernham Motorsports

CUP WINS: 44

2003 CUP EARNINGS: $4,321,190

CAREER EARNINGS: $73 million

No driver epitomizes NASCAR's growth in the 1980s more than Bill Elliott. This somewhat shy Georgia native dominated the sport during this time, and he helped NASCAR reach the next level in the public eye.

Elliott's star shone brightest in 1985, when he won a record 11 races and the inaugural Winston Million, a special short race for winners of the previous season. He also won a $1 million bonus from series sponsor R. J. Reynolds for winning the Daytona 500, the Southern 500 at Darlington and the Winston 500 at Talladega all in the same season. Elliott became known as "Million Dollar Bill" and "Awesome Bill from Dawsonville."

A short-track racer with a determination to get into NASCAR's big leagues, Elliott's experience on the bullrings gave him an understanding of car set-ups and adjustments needed to run competitively. He drove for an underfinanced family-team effort starting in 1976 with eight Cup races, and over the next six years the team struggled – to say the least – never placing higher than 25th in the standings.

Fortunes were about to change. With the financial backing of Michigan businessman Harry Melling, Elliott started winning. He won his first Cup race at Riverside in 1983, and the team placed third in points in 1983 and 1984.

For the next several years, Elliott and his Coors/Melling-sponsored Thunderbird became

a common sight in victory lane. The team was the first to get involved with Ford Motor Company at this time with the aerodynamically superior T-Bird, and this car was a rocket, especially on the superspeedways.

The competition were left scratching their heads as this red and white T-Bird dominated racing. Not only would Elliott win 11 races in 1985, he was so strong that NASCAR updated some rules to let the other teams play catch-up.

A prime example of the team's performance was Elliott's qualifying round at the 1985 Talladega race. He reached a record-breaking 209.398 miles per hour on the large 2.6-mile superspeedway.

Through these heady years, Elliott remained reserved and unassuming. He always spoke of his team's efforts and successes, and focused on the help of his brothers Dan and Ernie with the team. He just drove the car.

Elliott's success and modesty endeared him to the press and his ever-increasing legion of fans. He was NASCAR's most popular driver 16 times.

He won the Cup title in 1988 with six wins, six poles, 11 top-five and 22 top-10 finishes in 29 races. Elliott ended his relationship with Melling in 1991 and hooked up with Junior Johnson in 1992. This association proved fruitful, as he finished the 1992 season in second spot with five wins, and was only 10 points behind champ Alan Kulwicki.

Elliott, shown here at Rockingham in 2003, runs a limited schedule for Ray Evernham in 2004. He placed ninth in the 2003 standings.

Elliott (No. 9) and
Kenny Wallace zoom
by a pit lane worker at
Richmond in 2002.
Elliott was 16th.

Elliott leads the pack
at New Hampshire, July
2003. He placed 31st.

In 1995, Elliott started his own Cup team and ran with mixed results. Then in 2001 he announced a bombshell. He would join the newly formed Evernham Motorsports team as lead driver, competing in a Dodge, with the automaker returning to NASCAR after 20 years.

To prove he was still capable of the old magic, Elliott won the November 2001 race at Homestead-Miami, the first win for the new team. It was Dodge's first victory since Neil Bonnett won a NASCAR race in Ontario, Calif., in November 1977.

In 2002, Elliott won the Brickyard 400 at Indianapolis, and notched his 44th career win at the North Carolina Speedway in 2003.

As Elliott races in the 2004 Nextel Cup season – his 28th year – he quietly and modestly goes about his business. He is still a strong team player and gives credit to the entire team.

"It's not I. It's we," he said of his racing efforts. "It's all of us collectively putting this deal together week in and week out, and it's a great relationship."

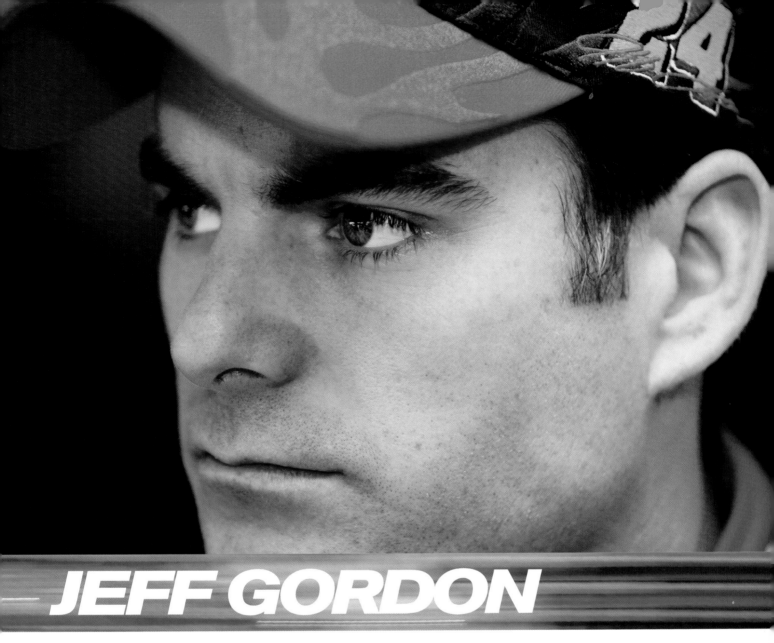

JEFF GORDON

It is a testament to Jeff Gordon's dazzling career that back-to-back fourth-place seasons constitute a huge slump.

Yet it should always be remembered that after one of the greatest four-year stretches in recent NASCAR history, Gordon finished sixth and ninth in the points standings before rebounding to win his fourth Cup title in 2001.

Many stock car fans have been quick to write Gordon off. He has never enjoyed the total admiration he should have for winning four Cup titles – putting him third behind legends Richard Petty and Dale Earnhardt – as well as two Daytona 500s, a record four straight Southern 500s and 64 Cup races overall.

Gordon, whose tight-knit team is known as the Rainbow Warriors because of their colorful uniforms, has even been booed by a large segment of the sport's fan base. He has been viewed as too corporate and too smooth. Reigning superstar Dale Earnhardt took a disliking to him and let everyone know about it. Plus, Gordon was from outside the south, had an open-wheel background and arrived with a huge and immediate impact. Too much, too soon, many fans thought.

"All my life I've been pushed to do things at a young age that nobody else had ever done before," Gordon said.

That is certainly true. When he was 4 years old, in Vallejo, Calif., Jeff's stepfather, John

NO. 24

BORN: **August 4, 1971, Vallejo, Calif.**

HOBBIES: **Skiing, golf, scuba diving**

TEAM: **Hendrick Motorsports**

CAR: **Chevrolet**

SPONSOR: **DuPont**

CUP WINS: **64**

2003 CUP EARNINGS: **$6,622,002**

CAREER EARNINGS: **$58,525,057**

Gordon at California Speedway, May 2004. It was the Rainbow Warrior's second straight Cup victory.

Bickford, bought him a Quarter Midget car. By the time he was 6, Gordon had won 35 main events and taken the Western States Championships. At 8, he won his first of Three-quarter Midget National Championships, and at 9 he won 46 of 50 events. Overall, he won more than 600 short-track races, including four national karting titles.

By the time he was 14, it was obvious that Gordon's future was in racing, and his parents moved to Pittsboro, Ind., where open-wheel racing is king, there are numerous tracks to hone a driver's skill and a younger driver could legally race Sprint Cars with parental permission. At 13, Gordon had already been behind the wheel of the 650-horsepower Sprints, and at 16, he became the youngest person ever awarded a license with the USAC. He hit the wall in his first race, but learned quickly and

won over 100 races by the time he finished high school.

In 1990, when he was 19, Gordon became the youngest Midget champion in USAC history. That was a pivotal year for the rising star, because he attended the Buck Baker Driving School at North Carolina Motor Speedway and found his calling. He told his stepfather, "Sell everything. We're going stock car racing." He got into a Busch Series race later that year.

Gordon teamed up with car owner Bill Davis for the 1991 Busch Series season, had five top-five finishes, was 11th in the points standings and was named rookie of the year. The next season, he set a Busch Series record with 11 poles, won three races, each of them from the pole, placed in the top-five a total of 10 times, finished fourth in points and set a single-

season winnings record of $412,293.

Gordon's unlimited promise did not go unnoticed. Owner Rick Hendrick watched him win at Atlanta in March 1992 and recalled, "He came out of the turn with the back end hanging out. He just kept on going. He was on the ragged edge all day."

Hendrick signed him for NASCAR's premier series and got him into the 1992 season-ending Winston Cup race at Atlanta, where he finished 31st.

Gordon arrived with a splash in 1993, becoming the first rookie driver to win a qualifying race for the Daytona 500 in 30 years. He started third, finished fifth and with a 14th-place finish in points was named that season's Winston Cup Rookie of the Year.

He got his first win the following year, in the Coca-Cola 600, and also won the first Brickyard 400.

"I have a lot of great memories in Victory Lane but it would be hard for me to top that," he said. "That was such a huge victory and elevated me to a new level."

Gordon was eighth in series points in 1994, despite 10 DNFs, which gave him 21 over his first two seasons.

At the age of 24, he became the youngest premier series champion of the modern era, with seven wins, 23 top-10s and only three DNFs. That began a phenomenal four-year stretch during which Gordon won 40 races while taking three series points titles and finishing runner-up by a mere 37 points to teammate Terry Labonte.

In 1997, at age 26, he became the youngest driver to win the Daytona 500, and he became the youngest three-time points champion in 1998. That same year he tied Richard Petty, for a modern era record of 13 wins, tied the series mark with four straight wins and set a then-record of $9.3 million.

Despite winning seven races, Gordon slumped to sixth in the points race in 1999, and it was a huge blow when he lost crew chief Ray Evernham to Dodge's return to stock car racing. He dropped to ninth in 2000, his worst finish in six years, but top-10 finishes in 10 of the last 11 races foreshadowed a great 2001 comeback. He won six races, took his fourth title and broke his own record with $10.8 million in prize money.

The fourth-place finishes and three wins in each of the 2002 and 2003 seasons seemed like a big drop-off.

"A good/bad thing happened to us," Gordon said. "We won a lot of races and championships, and set the bar very high for ourselves. But I don't feel that I've peaked. We still have wins left in us."

Celebrating after his Atlanta win in 2003. Gordon placed fourth that year in the points championship with three wins.

Gordon told his stepfather, "Sell everything. We're going stock car racing."

ROBBY GORDON

NO. 31

BORN: January 2, 1969, Bellflower, Calif.

HOBBIES: Water-skiing, boating, mountain biking

TEAM: Richard Childress Racing

CAR: Chevrolet

SPONSOR: Cingular Wireless

CUP WINS: 3

2003 CUP EARNINGS: $4,157,064

CAREER EARNINGS: $10,226,426

If a vehicle has four tires and a steering wheel, Robby Gordon can race it – and win in it.

One of the most versatile drivers in the world, Gordon has captured NASCAR premier series races, CART races, the legendary Baja 1000, prestigious truck series titles and numerous off-road championships during his jam-packed career.

He's often raced several different kinds of cars in the same year and is best known for his repeated attempts to compete in the most prestigious close-wheeled race, the Indy 500 at the famed Brickyard, and the Coca-Cola 600 NASCAR race – both on the very same day. A couple of times (in 1997 and 2000) rain in

Indianapolis foiled that bid, but in 2002 and 2003, he was able to board a helicopter on the infield after the checkered flag at Indy, and through a short plane ride and another helicopter trip, arrive in time for the green flag at Charlotte. In 2002, he was an impressive eighth in the Indy 500 and 16th in the Coca-Cola 600. The next May, he was 22nd and 17th, respectively.

"To do 1,100 miles in a day is pretty tough," Gordon said, "but in Indianapolis I drive the car like a video game, if the car is well set-up. I've been able to adapt very quickly from one car to the next, hopefully not making too many mistakes.

"I just like to race. I knew at the age of 5 that

it was something I wanted to do."

Gordon grew up in California and has been behind the wheel as long as he can remember. His first job was raking up the chaff in the feedlot his father, Bob, owned, but he and his dad also worked together as a driving team. They won four off-road races together when the younger Gordon was 17, and three more the next season including the renowned and grueling Baja 1000.

By then, Robby Gordon was already getting a toehold in the racing world. At 16, he won the first off-road race he entered, co-driving with Frank Arciero, and also won his debut in the Mickey Thompson stadium series. And from 1986–89 he won four straight SCORE/HDRA

off-road racing championships, including a solo-drive victory in the 1989 Baja 1000.

"I'm just fortunate that I grew up racing off-road cars," he said. "It taught you a lot of car control."

Gordon put that control to use in a stunning variety of races. He began full-time racing in 1990, and won the pole in his first stock car superspeedway event, an ARCA race at Atlanta. He also won the 24 Hours of Daytona for Roush Racing, took three other IMSA GTO events, and won the SCORE/HDRA Heavy Metal off-road title.

Gordon moved into NASCAR's Cup series in 1991, with an 18th-place debut at the Daytona 500 for Junie Donlavey, but although he made a

A versatile driver, Robbie Gordon is shown up on two wheels at Watkins Glen. The Dodge Save Mart 350 at Infineon was one of two wins for the Chevy driver.

Gordon (No. 31) surrounded by Tony Stewart (No. 20) and Jimmie Johnson (No. 48) at Dover 2004. Gordon maintains a full racing schedule, running both NASCAR and CART.

"In Indianapolis I drive the car like a video game."

well-documented drive for Robert Yates in the team's first race after Davey Allison's death in 1993, he had only sporadic Cup appearances until 1997 when he drove 20 races for Felix Sabates.

That didn't mean he was idle, however. He raced a full CART season in 1993, driving for legendary A. J. Foyt, was named the most improved driver the next year and finished fifth in the CART points standings in 1995 while winning at Detroit and Phoenix.

He also won the 1996 SCORE off-road title, was second in the IROC series twice and kept up his life-long love affair with the Indy 500. He made his debut at Indy with a 27th-place finish in 1993, had top-five finishes the next two years, and led 33 laps near the end of the 1999 race, only to run out of fuel on the last lap, to finish fourth.

He tried his first NASCAR/Indy "double duty" in 1997, but rain pushed the closed-wheel race back to the next day and Gordon was running second when a cockpit fire on the 19th lap gave him second- and third-degree burns on his hands, wrist and thigh, which kept him out of racing for a month.

Gordon concentrated on CART racing until 2000 when he teamed with John Menard and Mike Held to enter his own car for 17 NASCAR races and one top-five finish.

He continued to drive CART but also raced for three different NASCAR teams in 2001. When Richard Childress Racing driver Mike Skinner had season-ending surgery in September, Gordon filled in. In November, in his 10th start for Childress, Gordon picked up his first Cup win by beating Jeff Gordon in the season finale at the New Hampshire 300.

"I race a lot of different cars but the Cup car has been the most difficult I've ever had to adapt to," Gordon said. "The balance changes so much as you go through its fuel load."

It was only in 2002 that Gordon finally competed in a full NASCAR season, with 20 starts and five top-10s for Childress. In 2003, he set himself up for a good season by winning the first qualifying race for the Daytona 500. He moved up to 16th in the drivers' points race and won twice, becoming just the fourth driver to sweep the road-course races at Sonoma and Watkins Glen. He had a string of six top-10s in eight summer races and also became just the third driver in racing history to lead laps in both the Indy 500 and the Brickyard 400. Of course, he still competed in some off-road events.

"Doesn't matter if it's a trophy truck or a golf cart," Gordon said. "I just like to race."

KEVIN HARVICK

If you want something done well, ask a busy man – and you won't find many stock car drivers with a more crowded schedule than Kevin Harvick's.

Harvick raced in the Busch, Winston Cup and Craftsman Truck series from 2001–2003, and did well in all of them.

"Racing is my life," said the straight-speaking native of Bakersfield, Calif. "For some reason, the busier I am at the track, the better I tend to race. I think it's because I don't have to deal with all the distractions outside the car that can get me in trouble at times."

That trouble included probation, suspension or fines from NASCAR officials in each of his first three Cup seasons.

While Harvick, whose nickname is "Happy," has a reputation for always speaking his mind, he is best known for the unenviable task of taking over Dale Earnhardt's ride after the legend's death at the Daytona 500 in 2001. Although Richard Childress Racing changed the Chevrolet's number from 3 to 29 and its basic color from black to white, Harvick was still regarded as the man who replaced Earnhardt.

Harvick had often driven the No. 3 car in test runs when Earnhardt was busy, but his start at Rockingham, the race after Earnhardt's death, was his first on the premier series. The next month he edged Jeff Gordon by 0.006 seconds at Atlanta for a win in his third career start – a record at the time.

NO. **29**

BORN: **December 8, 1975, Bakersfield, Calif.**

HOBBY: **Radio-controlled cars**

TEAM: **Richard Childress Racing**

CAR: **Chevrolet**

SPONSOR: **GM Goodwrench**

CUP WINS: **4**

2003 CUP EARNINGS: **$6,237,119**

CAREER EARNINGS: **$14,388,537**

The car number may be changed from 3 to 29, but "Happy" Harvick has big boots to fill.

That set the tone for one of the most brilliantly varied seasons in recent history as he later won the inaugural race at Chicagoland Speedway, finished ninth in total points and was named rookie of the year. He also won the Busch Series, and had one drive in the Craftsman Truck Series. He competed in 69 races at 30 different tracks in NASCAR's top three series, covering over 20,000 racing miles.

"I've been pretty much bred to drive, and it started when I was 5 years old," he said.

When he finished his kindergarten year, Harvick's parents bought him a go-kart to race at local tracks, and over the next decade he won seven national titles and two Grand National championships. In 1992, while he was in high school, he switched to driving part-time on the Featherlite Southwest Series, and the next year won the Late Model title at Mesa Marin Raceway in his hometown. In 1995, he was rookie of the year in NASCAR's Elite Division Featherlite Southwest Series, finishing 11th in points.

In 1997, he decided to focus on racing full-time. In 1998, he won the NASCAR Grand National Winston West Series Championship, and the next year he drove in the Craftsman Truck Series, with 11 top-10 finishes. Childress liked his hard-charging style and gave him a ride in the tough Busch Series.

He was the Busch Rookie of the Year in 2000, winning three races and finishing third in points, and was looking forward to a run at the

Busch title in 2001 when he was suddenly promoted to "The Show" after Earnhardt's death. It was a spectacular debut season, as he became the first driver to win a Busch title and Cup rookie of the year.

Harvick had a sophomore slump in 2002. He dropped to 21st in points and had six DNFs, but he took the checkered flag at Chicagoland again. He also won his first Craftsman Truck race in his 785th start to become one of just five drivers to win races in all three of NASCAR's national series. However, he was also put on probation for an encounter with Greg Biffle after a Busch race, and when he spun another driver in a truck race three weeks later he was suspended for one Cup race.

"To me you should always speak your mind," Harvick said of his fiery attitude. "With me, you're going to get an honest answer and you're not going to get a bunch of bull in the middle of it."

Harvick got back on track in 2003, as Todd Berrier took over as crew chief in March. He finished fifth in series points, had a career best in top-five finishes (11) and top-10s (18), won the pole and the race in the 10th anniversary of the Brickyard 400 and also won three Busch Series races in 19 starts. He and Berrier seem destined for a Nextel Cup Series points championship.

"We just have to take that next little step," Harvick said."

In the No. 29 car, Harvick had some problems at Lowe's Motor Speedway in 2002, won one race and finished 21st, but came right back in 2003, ending up in fifth.

DALE JARRETT

NO. 88

BORN: November 26, 1956, Hickory, N.C.

HOBBY: Golf

TEAM: Robert Yates Racing

CAR: Ford

SPONSOR: UPS

CUP WINS: 31

2003 CUP EARNINGS: $4,121,487

CAREER EARNINGS: $41,818,270

Golf's loss is stock car racing's gain.

By birthright, Dale Jarrett seemed destined to follow his famous father onto the nation's top racing tracks, but it took a while for destiny to play its hand.

The son of two-time NASCAR Cup points champion Ned, Jarrett was a late-bloomer behind the wheel. He concentrated on other sports until he was 20 years old, when he and a couple of buddies put together a car for Jarrett to drive in the Limited Sportsman Division at Hickory Motor Speedway, his hometown track in North Carolina. In his first race, Jarrett started 25th, finished ninth and decided then and there that he wanted to race for a living.

Before that, he was the outstanding quarter-back on the football team, the star forward in basketball and a terrific shortstop on the base-ball team at his high school in Hickory.

"I knew he'd be a pro athlete, but I thought he'd be a pro golfer more than anything else," Ned Jarrett once said of his son.

In fact, the younger Jarrett turned down a golf scholarship at the University of South Carolina even though it was his favorite sport. Instead, he took a job doing odds and ends at the Hickory track, where his father had once been a race promoter.

"Every day during lunch, I'd set up my little driving range behind the racetrack and hit balls into an empty parking lot," Jarrett recalled.

While still an exceptional golfer, Jarrett has

nevertheless become one of stock car racing's all-time greats. Despite a dismal 26th-place finish in the points standings in 2003, the worst of his 18-year career, Jarrett won the second race of the season and now has won at least one Cup race in 11 straight seasons, seven back of Richard Petty's all-time record.

Along the way, he enjoyed an incredible six-year streak of top-five finishes in Cup points standings, capped by the series championship in 1999. That made the Jarretts only the second father/son team to capture racing's top points prize (Lee and Richard Petty were the first).

Jarrett began making his mark on the national scene when NASCAR formed the Busch Series in 1982, and he was a charter member. By 1984, he was fourth in Busch standings and had started to earn some drives in the premier series.

He won 11 Busch races and 14 poles before leaving the series for good in 1999, but his career on the major circuit was proceeding slowly. He drove for eight different owners from 1984 to 1989, and had only two top-five finishes.

But in 1990, the Wood Brothers hired Jarrett to replace Neil Bonnett in their renowned No. 21 car, and he recorded six top-10 finishes in the second half of the season. The next season, he broke a 134-start drought for the Woods with his first victory, at Michigan, and finished 17th in the points championship.

Dale Jarrett, shown here passing Larry Foyt at Atlanta in 2003, had a miserable year, ranking 26th at the end of the season.

Jarrett won the Pepsi 400 at Michigan in 2002. With two Cup victories that year, he placed ninth in the standings.

"I'm a believer that things are brought to you when you're ready for them."

When football coach Joe Gibbs started a NASCAR team in 1992, he hired Jarrett as his first driver. Jarrett finished 19th in the points race, but the next year he started the season by winning the Daytona 500, which Gibbs still calls the thrill of his racing career. It also propelled Jarrett into the sport's elite, and started his win-per-season streak, as he leapt all the way to fourth in points. He raced one more year for Gibbs before switching to Robert Yates, who needed a replacement for Ernie Irvan, badly injured at Michigan the previous season. He won the Daytona 500 pole and the checkered flag at Pocono on the way to a 13th-place finish.

Then Jarrett and Yates went into overdrive. In 1996, they won the Daytona 500 again, as well as three other races, and finished third in points. Jarrett was second the next year with a career-high seven victories, and was third again in 1998. Then came the championship in 1999, with a whopping 24 top-five finishes, four victories and Driver of the Year honors from every poll that really matters.

The late-bloomer had finally bloomed.

"My racing career has been a struggle because I never had any money, so it has been one slow step at a time," Jarrett said. "But I'm a believer that things are brought to you when you're ready for them. It's just taken me a long time to be ready for this."

Jarrett maintained his lofty standing when he was fourth in points in 2000 and fifth in 2001, a year in which he won three races in four starts early in the season. He had a chance to win the drivers' championship but six mid-season finishes of 30 or worse did him in. In 2000, he also won the Daytona 500 again, this time from the pole.

But the team dropped to ninth in points standings in 2000, their first drop out of the top-five in six years. Then came the dreadful 26th place in 2001, which included eight DNFs, Jarrett's highest total in a decade. He went through three crew chiefs before Mike Ford returned from Evernham Motorsports in 2004.

Jarrett said 2003 "was probably the longest year I can remember, but it's over now. We've put it behind us. You make changes, and it takes time. But having had success and being able to look back on it, this makes you appreciate that successful part of your career even more."

JIMMIE JOHNSON

It has to worry the world's top stock car drivers that Jimmie Johnson and his team are really just getting started.

"If you look at history, it takes three, four, five years to get the team and driver and everybody into championship form," the California native said after a superbly consistent 2003 season. "Maybe we'll have that special year soon."

Johnson finished second in the points race behind Matt Kenseth in 2003, the highest finish by a sophomore driver on NASCAR's top circuit since the late Dale Earnhardt took the Winston Cup Series title in 1980. Had the back-end-heavy points system which NASCAR adopted for the 2004 Nextel Cup Series been in place for the final Winston Cup run in 2003,

Johnson might well have been the champion. He wrapped up the year with an impressive six consecutive races in which he finished either second or third and jumped from fifth to second overall.

At the end of the season he was riding a streak of 69 straight weeks in NASCAR's top-10, the ninth longest streak in the premier series' modern era, nudging in behind names like Waltrip and Earnhardt.

"It's crazy," Johnson said at the end of the 2003 season. "It's amazing to me. I cannot believe we've been able to do it and my name is going to be alongside some of those greats I've looked up to my whole life."

One of the greats he surpassed in 2003 was

NO. **48**

BORN: **September 17, 1975, El Cajon, Calif.**

HOBBIES: **Water sports**

TEAM: **Hendrick Motorsports**

CAR: **Chevrolet**

SPONSOR: **Lowe's**

CUP WINS: **6**

2003 CUP EARNINGS: **$7,745,530**

CAREER EARNINGS: **$11,656,118**

Johnson spinning during the Nextel All-Star Challenge in May 2004. Not a common sight – as of July 2004 the Lowe's Chevy driver had three Cup wins and was leading the points race after 15 events.

his teammate at Hendrick Motorsports, Jeff Gordon, who owns the car Johnson drives. The employee upstaged the boss when he went head-to-head with the four-time Cup winner and passed him at The Winston, a non-points but very prestigious all-star race at Charlotte.

"If Jeff is going to get passed, I'm sure he'd want it to be the car he owns and is a teammate of," Johnson said, smiling. "So it was a lot of fun."

Johnson took the rain-shortened Coca-Cola 600 on the same track the very next week, and also swept both New Hampshire events to place himself squarely in the middle of NASCAR's "next generation" with the likes of Kenseth, Dale Earnhardt Jr., Ryan Newman and Kevin Harvick.

The others in that group expected to inherit the Nextel Series leaders' torch could have been anticipated, but Johnson's immediate success at the sport's upper level flew in under the radar. He went from a relative unknown to stardom in a matter of months.

Johnson is one of those rare athletes who make a bigger splash in the big leagues than they did in the minors, although there was nothing shabby about his developing years. He began racing in motocross at the age of 4 and credits his mother and father with being supportive but not pushy, which allowed him to enjoy the competition without the crushing pressure to win every week.

He migrated toward off-road racing rather

than stock cars, and became the youngest competitor in the history of the Thompson Stadium Truck Series. He won that title three straight years (1992–94) and took three other major off-road titles: the 1994 SCORE desert racing championship and the 1996 and 1997 SODA Winter Series championships.

In 1998, Johnson moved into stock cars and was rookie of the year in the ASA Challenge Series. He finished third in the ASA points race the next year, and also got five rides in the NASCAR Busch Series, including one top-10 finish. In 2000, his first full season in the Busch Series, he had six finishes in the top-10, and was 10th in the points standings. Driving for Herzog Motorsports, he moved up to eighth in the Busch Series. In 72 Busch races from 1998 to 2001, which included just two full seasons, Johnson won over $1.5 million.

In Johnson's final year on the Busch circuit, Rick Hendrick gave him three starts in the Winston Cup Series. His best finish in those three 2001 starts was 25th at Homestead-Miami – decent enough, but it in no way foretold what was to happen the next year.

Johnson began 2002 by winning the pole at the Daytona 500. He was only the third rookie in the modern era to take the 500 pole and did it in fewer starts (four) than the others. Loy Allen's 1994 pole came in his sixth race and Mike Skinner's 1997 pole start was his 16th career race.

Nine starts later, appropriately at California, Johnson had his first Cup win. He also took both checkered flags at Dover, becoming the first rookie to sweep both races at a single venue in the same season. He finished fifth in series points, and third in a very strong rookie field which also included Raybestos Rookie leader Ryan Newman, and Kurt Busch, who was third in points.

Perhaps the most significant event of Johnson's full-season debut was not one of his three victories but a third-place finish at Atlanta Motor Speedway in March. That vaulted him into the top-10 for the first time, and at the end of the next season he was still there. He even led the Series for one week in September before faltering.

He would not falter late in 2003, however, as he won three races and finished second overall. Three DNFs probably cost him the title, but he is philosophical about that.

"Every driver has a bunch of 'what ifs' in a season," Johnson said. "The guy who at the end of the year has the shortest list of 'what ifs' is the champion. Being the first loser doesn't bother me too bad. I didn't expect to be in this position."

A couple of years earlier, no one else expected it either.

Johnson leading Hendrick Motorsports teammate Jeff Gordon. Johnson moved to stock cars in 1998 after successful off-road racing campaigns.

Johnson's immediate success at the sport's upper level flew in under the radar. He went from a relative unknown to stardom in a matter of months.

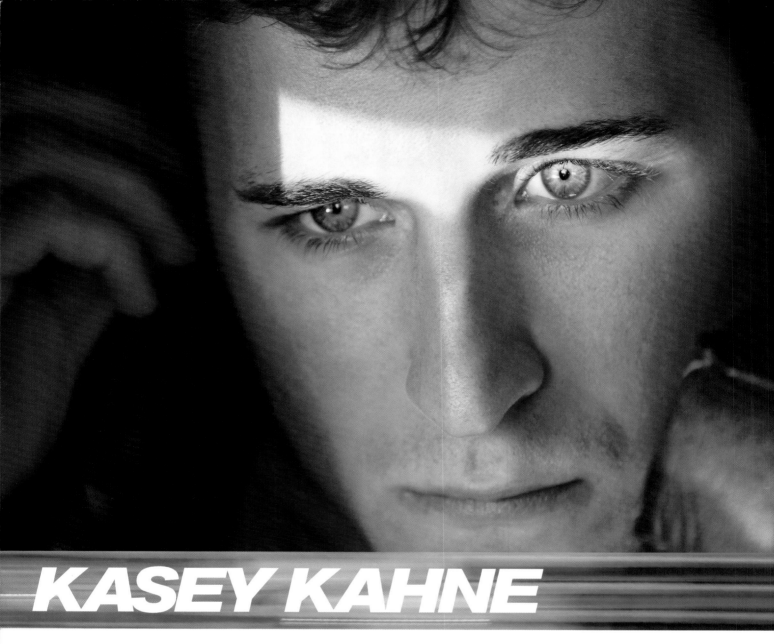

KASEY KAHNE

NO. 9

BORN: April 10, 1980, Enumclaw, Wash.

HOBBY: Racing open-wheel cars

TEAM: Evernham Motorsports

CAR: Dodge

SPONSOR: Dodge Dealers/UAW

When NASCAR realizes its ambition to have a Nextel Cup stop in the Pacific Northwest, there will be a hometown star to market.

Kasey Kahne has rapidly made a name for himself, despite moving into NASCAR's premier series only in 2004. The native of Enumclaw, Wash. – a town outside Tacoma, in the shadow of the Cascade Mountains – got off to a tremendous start in his rookie season, becoming just the seventh driver in Cup history to record top-five finishes in three of the first four starts of his career. By the time the season was seven races old, he had won two poles and finished second twice, including a 0.02 second loss to Elliott Sadler in the April race at Texas,

the eighth-closest finish in championship history – heady stuff for a guy just approaching his 24th birthday.

While Kahne's sudden impact was stunning, it was not totally unexpected by industry insiders. Kahne had been heavily courted by Evernham Motorsports to drive their No. 9 Dodge, replacing legend Bill Elliott who was moving into semi-retirement. They liked the manner in which Kahne had driven – and won – at almost every level, although he was just beginning to taste success in the Busch series.

When he moved into the sport's top series in 2004, Kahne had only two full seasons of stock car racing under his belt. Prior to that, he was a promising young star in open-wheel racing.

For instance, in 2001, he repeated as champion of the "Night Before the 500" Classic at Indianapolis Raceway Park, the first time the event had a back-to-back champion in the 11 years since Jeff Gordon accomplished the feat. Prophetically, when Kahne signed with legendary car owner Steve Lewis to run a full USAC schedule of Sprint, Midget and Silver Crown Series cars in 2000, Lewis often introduced him as "the next Jeff Gordon." Lewis has a good eye for future stardom: He has also fielded cars for the likes of Gordon, Tony Stewart and Ryan Newman.

Kahne was a long way, figuratively and literally, from that cream of the stock car crop when he was growing up in the state of Washington.

He began competing on Washington's dirt tracks and won four Micro-midget races in his first year at the wheel. As he has done as a full-time pro, he moved up quickly, winning 11 of the 14 races, the Hannigan Speedway Championship and the Northwest Mini-sprint Car title when he was 16 years old. In 1998, he was into full-sized Sprint cars and won a dozen times.

By 2000, he was competing full-time in USAC events for Lewis and also raced limited schedules in the Toyota Atlantic Series and Formula Ford 2000 Series before jumping over to the NASCAR Busch Series. He spent his rookie year driving for Robert Yates in 2002, his sophomore campaign with Akins Motorsports.

"When I came over, I looked at it as a tough

Rookie sensation Kasey Kahne on the hook after spinning in oil at Dover in June 2004, placing 21st. After 15 races of the 2004 season, he has amassed four second-place finishes.

"The biggest thing I know is how easy it is to get in trouble and not finish the race."

series and it actually was even tougher than I thought it would be," Kahne said. "Lots of drivers in open-wheel respect stock cars, but there's others that think driving a stock car is pretty easy. I kind of enjoy the ones that think it's easy. Then they go out and try it and see how hard it really is."

Kahne finished seventh in the Busch drivers standings in 2003, but didn't land his first win until the final event of the year at Homestead.

"I really didn't think it would take so long," Kahne said. "It did take almost two years, but I learned a lot in all that time and it actually felt that much better when we finally did win a race. It was more a relief than anything, I think.

"I learned a lot of things in the Busch Series, a lot of good things and bad things, things to do and things not to do. The biggest thing I know is how easy it is to get in trouble and not finish the race."

Kahne had expected to spend another full season in Busch, but Ray Evernham had different ideas. While Kahne has arrived in the Nextel Cup Series with a splash, he doesn't think such early success will adversely affect his development.

"I don't think it hurts my learning curve," he said. "I'm just trying not to lose focus. It's been a dream to get the support and help from Bill Elliott. Bill, Dale Jr. and Jeremy Mayfield have given me some advice on all of this. I went from having not much media contact to a bunch every week. It's changed a lot, but it's changed for a good reason.

"And it all makes for more fans watching NASCAR in the Pacific Northwest."

MATT KENSETH

As Matt Kenseth crossed the finish line at North Carolina Speedway in early November 2003, his Roush Racing team broke into a wild celebration. He didn't win the Pop Secret Microwave Popcorn 400, but Kenseth's fourth-place finish was good enough to capture the Winston Cup points championship.

It was appropriate that Bill Elliott won the race on Kenseth's big day because it was as Elliott's emergency replacement that Kenseth had made his debut on the Winston Cup five years earlier. It was also fitting that Kenseth did not win the race that clinched him the title in just his fourth full year on the elite NASCAR circuit, because his championship season was less about winning than coming close. He had stood atop the points race for seven months, not by taking checkered flags – he only won once in the entire season – but by turning in an amazingly consistent string of performances.

Kenseth had 11 top-five finishes and a stunning 26 top-10 finishes, but his only 2003 victory was at the UAW-DaimlerChrysler 400. In his breakthrough season the year before, he won a series-high five races, but finished only eighth in the final standings.

"When we got done (in 2002) we felt like we had a great year," Kenseth said. "But we had some bad days that were real bad. We were hoping we'd learn from the mistakes we made. But we felt like we had all the tools to put

NO. **17**

BORN: **March 10, 1972, Cambridge, Wis.**

HOBBIES: **Motorcycles, golf, boating**

TEAM: **Roush Racing**

CAR: **Ford**

SPONSOR: **DeWalt Power Tools**

CUP WINS: **7**

2003 CUP EARNINGS: **$4,038,120**

CAREER EARNINGS: **$12,222,092**

Kenseth at speed at California Speedway in 2003, the year he won the Cup title.

Opposite: Pumped and triumphant after his Checker Auto Parts 500 win at Phoenix in 2002.

together a strong season. It had been a dream."

It was a dream that started in the family, as so many stock car dreams do. Kenseth was raised in Cambridge, Wis., and when he was 13 his father, Roy, made a deal with his son. Roy would buy a race car and drive it competitively if Matt would work on it. When Matt was 16, he could get behind the wheel and compete on the demanding Wisconsin stock car scene.

That early training contributed to Kenseth's sensitive touch behind the wheel. "Matt probably was better than most as far as his seat-of-the-pants feel," said Wisconsin racing legend Steve Holzhausen. "He would get out of the car and say maybe he needed a softer shock on the right front or a stiffer spring on the right rear. A

lot of guys would have to lean on their crew chief to get a car right."

That knowledge became evident as Kenseth began his early rise up the tough ranks of Midwest short tracks. Although Kenseth is now regarded as one of the most soft-spoken NASCAR drivers – "He's about as controversial as a librarian," one observer said – around Wisconsin tracks in the late 1980s and early 1990s, he was known as "Matt the Brat." He was young, talented and anxious to succeed.

And succeed he did. By the age of 19, Kenseth had moved to Late Model ranks and became the youngest feature winner in the history of the ARTGO Challenge Series, breaking the record set by his current team member Mark

The DeWalt crew whoops it up at Michigan in 2002, Kenseth's third of five wins that year.

Kenseth is regarded as one of the most soft-spoken NASCAR drivers. "He's about as controversial as a librarian."

Martin. At 21, he was the youngest driver ever to win the prestigious Oktoberfest ARTGO race, which gained him national attention. At 23, he won track titles at both Madison International Speedway and Wisconsin International Raceway, and set another youngest-winner-ever mark at the Miller Genuine Draft National Championship. In 1996, he finished third in the demanding Hooters Series.

Kenseth started 1997 by driving for Gary Gunderman in the American Speed Association and was in second place in April when a call came from Robbie Reiser to join Reiser Enterprises on the NASCAR Busch Grand National Series. Despite making only 21 starts, he finished second in the rookie standings.

In 1998, Kenseth had three Busch wins and 17 top-five finishes on the way to a second-place standing behind Dale Earnhardt Jr., kick-starting their head-to-head rivalry. Most importantly, he got his first drive on the elite Winston Cup Series in September when he was asked to substitute for Bill Elliott. He finished a remarkable sixth.

He earned five more Winston Cup starts for Roush Racing in 1999, and also won four Busch Series races, but finished third in the points standings behind Earnhardt Jr. Both Kenseth and Earnhardt Jr. jumped to the elite Winston

Cup in 2000, but it was Kenseth who took the Rookie of the Year title with 11 top-10 finishes and became the first rookie to win the Coca-Cola 600 at Lowe's Motor Speedway.

Kenseth and his team suffered a slight sopho-more jinx in 2001, finishing 13th in the points standings, but finished strong with three fourth-place finishes in the season's last six races. That set the stage for a mercurial 2002, when Kenseth began to show his potential greatness. He captured a series-high five Winston Cup races and finished eighth in the standings.

In 2003, Kenseth grabbed the points lead on the fourth weekend and held onto it all alone until clinching the title on the second Sunday of November. Kenseth joined the late Alan Kulwicki as the only champions from Wisconsin. But he's not going to rest on his laurels.

"You can never be too confident, because I know how quickly this sport can change on you," said Kenseth. "Anything can happen at any given time."

BOBBY LABONTE

Bobby Labonte went from sweeping floors for his older brother to joining him as a champion of stock car racing's most prestigious series.

When Labonte won the 2000 Winston Cup points championship, he and Terry (the 1984 and 1996 winner) became the only brothers to capture NASCAR's elite title. It marked a long, steady climb from 1982 when, at the age of 19, Bobby was doing menial work in Terry's shop at Hagan Racing.

"Sure, I'm proud of it," Labonte said of the siblings' place in racing history. "When I was younger and watching Terry race, I thought about us racing against each other and maybe competing for a championship."

Seven years younger than Terry, Bobby started racing Quarter Midgets in Corpus Christi, Tex., when he was 5 years old. When he was 14, he shifted to go-karts, but the family soon moved to North Carolina to help with Terry's rising racing career.

The younger Labonte eventually moved from the broom to the pits with Hagan Racing, and Terry was the driver. While he worked on the crew Bobby moonlighted, working on his own Late Model stock cars. When Terry left Hagan for Junior Johnson after the 1986 season Bobby, naturally, was fired.

"I thought, 'Since I've got all this time on my hands, I might as well work on my own car and run some more races,'" Labonte said. He was

NO. 18

BORN: May 8, 1964, Corpus Christi, Tex.

HOBBY: Fishing

TEAM: Joe Gibbs Racing

CAR: Chevrolet

SPONSOR: Interstate Batteries

CUP WINS: 21

2003 CUP EARNINGS: $5,505,018

CAREER EARNINGS: $35,641,747

working for car builder Jay Hedgecock and also racing Late Model stocks at Caraway Speedway in Asheboro and was talented enough to win the 1987 track championship with 12 checkered flags in 23 starts. He moved up to the Sportsmen's Series at Concord and by 1990 was racing a full NASCAR Busch Series schedule, finishing fourth.

Labonte won the 1991 Busch Series championship and felt confident enough to make his debut in the premier series, the Winston Cup, with his own car. He entered two races as an owner/driver with mediocre results.

He lost the 1992 Busch points championship by three points to Joe Nemechek, the closest race in the history of NASCAR's three national series championships, but had shown enough that he landed a full-time ride with Bill Davis Racing for the Winston Cup Series.

He finished 19th in series points as a rookie in 1993, beginning a seven-year climb toward the top rung of the ladder. In 1994, he had two top-10 finishes and made his first entry into the top-five, with a fifth at Watkins Glen, but finished 21st in points. It would be the last year he failed to win a premier series race.

After the 1994 season, Labonte left Davis and moved to Joe Gibbs Racing, replacing the venerable Dale Jarrett in the No. 18 car. It was a career-making move as he finished 10th in points and won three races, his first career victory coming at the Coca-Cola 600 in Char-

lotte. He also swept the two Michigan events.

He won the season finale at Atlanta in 1996, the same day Terry clinched his second Winston Cup Series championship. And in 1997 and 1998, Bobby primed for his own run at the title by finishing seventh and sixth in points, winning three times and harvesting 36 top-10 finishes.

In 1999, Labonte finished second by 201 points to Jarrett, the man he replaced at Joe Gibbs Racing, establishing all kinds of career bests in the process. Despite breaking his shoulder blade in a Busch Series practice session, he won five times, including his third straight win at Atlanta, and had top-five finishes 23 times.

That set the stage for his remarkable 2000 season when Labonte took the points lead after the third race and dropped out of the lead just once all season. He won four races, had just two finishes outside the top 20 and failed to complete just nine laps out of 10,167 to beat Dale Earnhardt by 265 points for the Winston Cup title.

"When I see Bobby up front in the top-five most of the time, it makes me feel good," brother Terry said at the time. "I've seen him become a real thinking driver."

Labonte dropped to sixth overall the next season, but won at Pocono and, again, Atlanta. Then in 2002, he suffered a setback by finishing 16th, the second-worst of his career. Michael McSwain was brought in as crew chief, and the team switched from Pontiac to Chevrolet Monte Carlo for the 2003 season with immediate results.

He went from five top-five finishes to 12, from seven top-20s to 17, and if not for a terrible seven-race stretch which included a crash and two engine failures, he would have finished much higher than seventh. He won two races, including the final race of the Winston era at Homestead-Miami, indicating that his down year in 2002 was a blip, not a trend.

"The goal at this point in time is to become a multi-champion," Labonte said.

Just like older brother.

Labonte gets tires and fuel in the Auto Club 500 at California Speedway, April 2003. He took second place.

Opposite: Labonte at California Speedway, 2003. From sweeping floors to NASCAR champ, Labonte won four races and the title in 2000.

TERRY LABONTE

NO. **5**

BORN: **November 16, 1956, Corpus Christi, Tex.**

HOBBIES: **Hunting, fishing**

TEAM: **Hendrick Motorsports**

CAR: **Chevrolet**

SPONSOR: **Kellogg's**

CUP WINS: **22**

2003 CUP EARNINGS: **$4,283,625**

CAREER EARNINGS: **$34,064,557**

Two important things about Terry Labonte as a stock car racer: First, he finishes what he starts, and second, it's never wise to count him out, even when he looks like he'll never get back in again.

Labonte, nicknamed "The Iceman" because he seldom, if ever, blows his cool, has been in races totaling nearly a quarter-million laps and has managed to complete a phenomenal 90 percent of them. Entering the 2004 season, Labonte was riding a streak of 45 straight races without a DNF, not far off his Hendrick Motorsports teammate Jeff Gordon's record of 56.

In 1996, a dozen years removed from his Cup points championship racing for Billy Hagan,

Labonte won the title again under the Hendrick banner. In 2003, after five years out of the top-10, Labonte collected just enough points in the season's final race to again crack the top-10 elite. That same autumn, more than four years removed from his previous Cup victory, Labonte won the final Southern 500 to be contested on Labor Day weekend.

Both of these career recoveries came in the year he turned 48, and they delighted a legion of NASCAR fans. One of the sport's truisms is that nobody roots against Terry Labonte, one of the most gentlemanly drivers in the game.

There was a nice symmetry to his 2003 comeback win at the Southern 500. He made his first-ever Cup appearance at the unique

Darlington oval in 1978, had his first victory there on September 1, 1980, and then got that confidence-injecting victory at Darlington on the 2003 Labor Day weekend.

Very few NASCAR drivers have ever earned more respect among their peers than Labonte. He began his hall-of-fame career at the age of 7 in Corpus Christi, Tex., winning Quarter Midget races. By the time he had turned 16, he moved into stock cars, at first owned by his father, Bob, and then by Billy Hagan.

"My big break came several years ago when I was racing in Houston, Tex., and I met Billy Hagan," Labonte said. "He started sponsoring my short-track car, and he asked me if I wanted to go racing in his Winston Cup car a few times."

In the late 1970s, the Labonte family moved to North Carolina so Terry could be closer to NASCAR competition. In 1978, he got his first rides for Hagan, and although he drove only five Cup races that year, he placed in the top-10 in his first three, including his debut at fourth place in the Southern 500.

Labonte drove eight straight years, and 11 in all for Hagan, including a runner-up to Dale Earnhardt in the 1979 rookie of the year race, when he finished 10th in the points standings. That began a streak of seven consecutive seasons in the top-10.

He notched his first Cup win at Darlington in his sophomore season, while moving up to eighth in the points race. From there it was

One of NASCAR's most gentlemanly drivers, this Texan has been running Cup races since 1978. He is shown here just ahead of Dale Earnhardt Jr.

This shot of Labonte against the wall in the Pepsi 400 at Daytona in 2000 sums up a rough season, with no wins and averaging a 20th-place finish for the year.

fourth, third, fifth and finally the top of the list in 1984, when he racked up an impressive 17 top-five finishes. At 27, he was the youngest driver ever to win the NASCAR premier series.

He dropped to seventh in 1985 (although he won his first of 10 Busch Series races) and was down to 12th in 1986 before leaving Hagan for three years with Junior Johnson and another with Richard Jackson. He finished third, fourth and 10th in his three years with Johnson, and won the 1989 IROC title. He dropped to 15th with Jackson in 1990, the first time since 1982 that he didn't win a Cup race.

Labonte moved back to familiar territory in 1991, teaming with Hagan, but his career-low 18th in points standing and second successive winless season was entirely forgettable except for one thing: Labonte raced against his younger brother Bobby for the first time in NASCAR's premier series. Terry finished 24th and Bobby was 10 spots behind him.

In his three years back with Hagan, Labonte didn't win a race, but he also didn't miss any, and was building up a solid string of consecutive starts when Rick Hendrick hired him in 1994.

The collaboration with Hendrick paid immediate dividends. In 1994, Labonte won three races for the first time in his career and finished seventh in points. He won three different races in 1995 and also won a Craftsman Truck race at Richmond, one of his favorite tracks, to become just the fifth driver to win at least once in each of NASCAR's three national series.

Labonte won two races by early May 1996, and went on to record a career-high seven runner-up spots, add six more thirds and a total of 21 top-five finishes to become the fifth driver in the modern era to win multiple Cup titles. Teammate Jeff Gordon finished second, and Hendrick Motorsports' golden year was enhanced with Labonte's 514th consecutive career start at Martinsville in late April, eclipsing the record of the great Richard Petty.

Labonte had decent seasons in 1997 and 1998 with a couple of wins, but his five-year run of top-10 finishes ended in 1999 when he finished 12th in Cup points. Then in 2000, his streak of 655 consecutive starts was broken when he suffered dizziness after a crash at Daytona and was forced to miss two races.

When he finished 23rd in 2001, and 24th the next year, the doomsayers felt his career was all but done. Then came the rebound of 2003, and in typical Labonte fashion, he didn't gloat.

"It kind of put the retirement issue on the backburner," he said.

STERLING MARLIN

A journeyman NASCAR Cup driver and son of one of the sport's early prominent drivers, Sterling Marlin has never achieved superstar status in NASCAR's premium division, but he has always been a threat.

At 46 years of age, Marlin still hopes to win a coveted NASCAR championship. He came close in 2002, when he led the points race for 25 weeks of the season, but a neck injury put him out of contention with only seven races left.

"I am in a situation where I just go out to race to win every week," Marlin said.

"Twenty years ago, winning the points championship wasn't that big a deal. Now winning a championship is a very big deal, and that is our ultimate goal."

Marlin started working in the race shop of father Coo Coo Marlin when he was 12. By the time he was 16, he was his father's team's crew chief. In May 1976, he made his Cup debut after Coo Coo broke his shoulder and could not race.

Marlin ran his first full NASCAR season in 1983 with car owner Roger Hamby. He placed 19th in the standings and was named rookie of the year.

His first Cup win came a decade later in 1994 – and in fine fashion, as he won the season-opening Daytona 500 running for Morgan-McClure Motorsports. The win was his first in 279 starts. One year later Marlin won the

NO. 40

BORN: June 30, 1957, Franklin, Tenn.

HOBBIES: University football, U.S. Civil War history

TEAM: Chip Ganassi Racing

CAR: Dodge

SPONSOR: Coors Light

CUP WINS: 10

2003 CUP EARNINGS: $3,960,810

CAREER EARNINGS: $24 million

Top: Marlin gets the pit treatment at Texas Motor Speedway in April 2004.

Above: His Coors Light–sponsored car has interesting sponsor logo-graphics on car's bottom edge.

Opposite: Marlin at speed at Michigan 2003.

his 36 races that year, he had two wins, 12 top-fives, 20 top-10s and one pole.

In 2002, it appeared Marlin and his Dodge would win the title. He won the UAW-Daimler-Chrysler 400 and the Carolina Dodge Dealers 400 at Darlington. He stayed at the top of the points race for 25 weeks, but following his accident at Kansas Speedway, which resulted in fractured vertebrae, he was out for the rest of the year, placing 18th in points.

Healthy and ready for the 2003 season, Marlin reached a career milestone in October when he entered his 600th Cup race at Martinsville, but during the year he and his team suffered with a rash of mechanical gremlins and on-track incidents, including four DNFs. He once again placed 18th at the end of the season.

Marlin, now considered one of NASCAR's veteran drivers, plans to race as long as possible. He has spoken about the prize money over his career, noting in his first win at Nashville in 1976 he pocketed $565, and in 2000, he won close to $2 million.

He still believes he has a lot to offer in his racing career.

"I see myself driving fast for at least four or five years. The whole key for me to keep racing is to continue to be competitive. As long as I am competitive, I will stay in the sport."

Daytona 500 again after starting third; he is only the third driver to take back-to-back wins at Daytona, joining Richard Petty and Cale Yarborough.

In 1998, driving the Coors Light Chevrolet for Team SABCO, Marlin placed 13th in the Cup standings, but it wasn't until 2001 that he took another trip to the winner's circle, winning at Michigan and Lowe's Motor Speedway.

In fact, 2001 was Marlin's most successful season. Driving the then-new Dodge entry for Chip Ganassi Racing, he kept the No. 40 right in the hunt, and placed third in the points. Of

MARK MARTIN

NO. 6

BORN: January 9, 1959, Batesville, Ark.

HOBBIES: Flying, weight training

TEAM: Roush Racing

CAR: Ford

SPONSOR: Viagra

CUP WINS: 33

2003 CUP EARNINGS: $4,048,850

CAREER EARNINGS: $34 million

"I started racing cars when I was 15, even before I had a driver's license," said Mark Martin. "That's when I discovered everything about the sport of stock car racing thrilled me. I became obsessed with the sound and the speed, but mostly the prospect of becoming a successful driver someday."

Martin has succeeded, becoming one of the most prominent drivers on the Cup circuit.

Born in 1959, Martin took to the dirt tracks of his native Arkansas, winning his first race in only his third attempt behind the wheel. By 1976, he was racing on asphalt, and a year later entered the short-track world of American Speed Association competition. Martin also did well in this venue, winning the ASA crown in

three consecutive years from 1978 to 1980.

Martin started his NASCAR career in 1981, and has become one of its most successful drivers. Although he has never won the championship, he has placed second four times, and has amassed 33 Cup victories since 1988, running with Roush Racing, one of the sport's top teams.

He has been called a "racer's racer," and has always been a dominant force in Cup racing. If it's at all possible, Martin will use his skill and expertise to put his Ford in victory lane.

His early NASCAR efforts were meager and without success. He funded and drove for himself starting in 1981, and ran five races. He ran a full season in 1982, placing 14th in the

standings. With no financing, however, Martin sold his cars and equipment and raced a limited NASCAR schedule for the next few years for various teams. During this period he also went back to what he did best, racing ASA stock cars, where he claimed another championship in 1986 in the Midwest U.S.-based series.

After running in NASCAR's Busch Grand National Series in 1987, he got the attention of famed race car engine builder Jack Roush, who was preparing his own Cup team for 1988. Martin was signed to drive with the team.

The Roush-Martin collaboration succeeded almost immediately. Although 15th in the standings in their first year, the team took third spot in 1989 with a win at North Carolina Motor Speedway, 14 top-fives, 17 top-10s and five poles.

The chemistry between car owner and driver has been an important factor in their success.

"Jack Roush is, in my opinion, the best team owner in racing, and I also consider him my surrogate father since my father, Julian, died in a plane crash in 1998. Jack has looked out for me since we teamed up, and we've been together ever since, through the good times and the bad times."

Martin has also commented that a relationship between a driver and an owner involves a lot of give and take, along with trust, adding he believes this is true with Roush. "Jack and I

Known as a "racer's racer," Martin, shown here at Homestead-Miami in 2002, has never won a Cup title since his start in 1981.

A year later at Homestead-Miami, Martin mixes it up with Ward Burton. He finished 17th in the 2003 standings.

Right: Martin gets the nod at Dover, June 2004. It was the Arkansas native's 33rd Cup win.

have similar approaches to dealing with the team and the race car. Over the years I've come to understand that Jack and I are similar in the way we do things, and we both care about making our team as good as possible so that Roush Racing can win its first championship."

So during this partnership, Martin has always

been on the hunt. In 1998, he won a career-best seven victories with 22 top-five and 26 top-10 finishes. During this nine-year period he was never lower than sixth in the standings on a yearly basis.

Martin has not been as successful since 1998, but since that time he did add four Cup wins to his credit, and placed second in Cup standings in 2002. For 2003, there were problems and he placed 17th in the points with no wins.

Martin is one of NASCAR's most recognizable personalities, and he appears regularly on television commercials, giving him a solid presence both on and off the racetrack. He went to the forefront in the public eye when the male sexual enhancement drug Viagra signed on as his car's major sponsor. He understands a presence off the track is important for promotion.

"When I began racing, I didn't want to talk that much, much less look into a camera for the entire world to see," he said. "As my career progressed, however, I figured out that being on TV was a great way to market myself, so I forced myself to get used to all that. Now, I don't even think about being nervous because I'm on TV. I just think about winning races."

So no matter what name is on the side of Martin's car, this cool veteran will always be in the thick of each weekly Cup race, with one goal in mind – to win races.

JEREMY MAYFIELD

As one of the three team drivers for Evernham Motorsports, Jeremy Mayfield's role as a NASCAR Nextel Cup driver is simple: win races.

Even though he is part of a team that includes rookie sensation Kasey Kahne and established veteran Bill Elliott, Mayfield believes he is in his best position for making his mark in Cup racing.

"This is by far the best situation I've been in," Mayfield said about his current ride in the No. 19 Dodge Dealers Intrepid fielded by Evernham. "I feel like this is it. I feel like this is a great situation."

This 35-year old Kentucky native is now in his 11th year of Cup competition, and signed on with the relatively new Evernham team in 2001.

He has come a long way from racing karts and BMX bikes around his hometown of Owensboro. Graduating to the regular Saturday night short-track scene in Nashville, Tenn., at 19, Mayfield went to work as a fabricator at Sadler Racing. His determination to race was noted by the Sadlers, who got him set up with an ARCA Series Late Model ride.

By 1987, Mayfield was performing well in ARCA racing, taking eight top-five and 10 top-10 finishes. By 1993, Earl Sadler prepared a Cup car, and Mayfield's first Cup effort at Charlotte Motor Speedway in October 1993 resulted in a 29th-place finish.

NO. 19

BORN: May 27, 1969, Owensboro, Ky.

HOBBY: Radio-controlled model cars

TEAM: Evernham Motorsports

CAR: Dodge

SPONSOR: Dodge Dealers/UAW

CUP WINS: 3

2003 CUP EARNINGS: $2,962,230

CAREER EARNINGS: $17 million

Mayfield (right) and Jamie McMurray get close and personal at Lowe's Motor Speedway in May 2004.

Opposite: Running in the Carolina Dodge Dealers 400 at Darlington in March 2004, Mayfield took ninth spot.

His up-and-coming talents were noticed by legendary driver turned car owner Cale Yarborough. This full-time ride in 1995 and 1996 gave Mayfield lots of experience but not much success, as he placed 31st and 26th, respectively.

In the next four years, he drove for Michael Kranefuss and Penske Racing with better results. He won his first Cup race, the Pocono 500 in June 1998, and finished a career-high seventh in the standings. With Penske he notched two more victories, the NAPA Auto Parts 500 and the Pocono 500, both won in 2000.

Now in his fourth season with Evernham, Mayfield has not achieved much success, and has not yet wheeled his Dodge into victory lane. Still, he believes the learning curve at Evernham is starting to pay dividends, and the entire team is focused and determined. As well, when a team driver like Kahne is doing well, the entire group effort benefits.

"There's no comparison," Mayfield said about his team's efforts between 2003 and 2004. "Last year we thought we were going to be good but still not sure. The confidence level was kind of there. This year going to Daytona it was a whole different world. We all believed in each other.

"This is the kind of year you look forward to and you can't wait to get back racing. You know your stuff will be right, and you know everybody is on the same page and headed in the same direction."

Mayfield also has high praise for car manufacturer Dodge.

"Dodge gives us a ton of support," he said. "It's unbelievable the difference between other manufacturers and their race team and Dodge and their race teams. Everybody at Dodge is excited."

After several years of driving in the background in Cup racing, Mayfield believes he has been given a great opportunity.

"It's a big deal and something I've been very blessed to be a part of and see how it's taken shape. It starts with Ray and Dodge. They're the ones that provide us with resources and things we need to race with, and it's been overwhelming to me."

JOE NEMECHEK

NO. 01

BORN: September 26, 1963, Lakeland, Fla.

HOBBIES: Fishing, skiing

TEAM: MB2 Motorsports

CAR: Chevrolet

SPONSOR: U.S. Army

CUP WINS: 3

2003 CUP EARNINGS:
$2,626,484

CAREER EARNINGS:
$14,982,115

Joe Nemechek knows what it's like to pay your dues to get to the big leagues – and what it's like to pay them again once you've been there a while.

"Back when I and a lot of other Winston Cup drivers came in, drivers had to get in something that wasn't so good, and prove themselves," the popular Florida native said, "and then make the next step, and the next step after that. Times have changed."

Yet, in some ways times haven't changed much at all. After a decade in NASCAR's premier series, Nemechek was forced to prove himself again to keep behind the wheel, as he had one team fold under him, another release

him because of sponsorship problems and a third hire him as a replacement for an injured driver who was promised a ride when he recovered.

Still, Nemechek takes it all in stride and keeps qualifying for good positions on the starting grid, a talent which has earned him the nickname "Front Row Joe."

"In this sport, you have to prove yourself every week," he said, "because you're only graded on your last performance."

Compared to most elite drivers, Nemechek got a late start in racing. His career actually began on two wheels, at the age of 13, when he took up competitive motocross. By the time he climbed off the bikes and into cars six years

later, he had won more than 300 trophies.

Then he started a 10-year climb to the elite division of stock car racing. Within four years, Nemechek had become savvy enough to wrack up a phenomenal three-year streak, winning both the driver's championship and rookie of the year in three different series. He took the double crown in Southeastern Mini-Stocks in 1987, the United Stock Car Alliance in 1988 and the All Pro Series in 1989.

Nemechek broke into NASCAR's Busch circuit in 1990 and, of course, was named rookie of the year in that series as well. The drivers' championship portion of the twin crown would have to wait, but not for long. In 1992, in the closest title race in the history of

NASCAR's three national series, he won the Busch Series championship by three points over Bobby Labonte. That year, as well as the next, he was named the most popular Busch driver, an honor that still means a lot to him.

After his 1992 title, he still drove in the Busch Series but was ready to throw his hand into a bigger ring. So, finally, on July 11, 1993, about two months before he turned 30 years old, Nemechek finally lined up on a NASCAR Cup starting grid. He was 36th in his debut at New Hampshire and raced five times that season, twice for Morgan-McClure and three under his own team ownership.

Larry Hendrick hired Nemechek to drive the full 1994 Cup season, and he had three top-10

Nemecheck's U.S. Army–sponsored Chevy is not only patriotic but one of the circuit's most popular cars.

This Florida driver ran with the Hendrick and MB2 Motorsports teams in 2003, but didn't have a great time at Dover in the MBNA American 400.

"In this sport, you have to prove yourself every week, because you're only graded on your last performance."

finishes, including a third at Pocono, and finished third in the rookie of the year race behind Jeff Burton.

Nemechek entered the Cup series as an owner/driver again in 1995 and 1996, but in 58 races he never finished higher than fourth and recorded only six top-10s.

So when Felix Sabates offered him a ride for the 1997 season he took it, while he and wife Andrea also kept their own team running in the Busch Series. He had three top-10 finishes, but qualified well, with the first two poles of his Cup career, and five front-row starts.

In 1999, his third year with Sabates, Nemechek dropped to 30th in the points standings, but he won a career-high three poles, and in his 180th career start he won his first Cup race. Appropriately, it came at New Hampshire, the very track where he'd made his first start in NASCAR's premier series.

Nemechek joined Andy Petree's team in 2000 and the relationship was an immediate hit. He jumped up to a career-best 15th in the points championship, and also had personal bests in top-10s (nine) and top-fives (three).

His second, and last, season with Petree wasn't as strong, as he dipped to 28th in series points. He still managed to ring up the second win of his career, in the November race at Rockingham.

Then came two years of uncertainty.

Nemechek began 2002 with Haas-Carter Motorsports, but that team stopped operation after seven starts because their sponsors had financial problems. Nemechek started the next race as an emergency replacement for Johnny Benson. He finished 12th. At the race after that, Rick Hendrick asked him to drive the No. 25 car after the company had released Jerry Nadeau.

Nemechek finished out 2002 and raced the first 32 events of 2003 for Hendrick Motorsports before the team released him. In the middle of that turmoil, he picked up his third career victory, starting second, leading 156 laps and taking the checkered flag at Richmond in May. A month later, he reached a personal milestone with his 300th career start, at Pocono.

Nadeau's misfortune was again Nemechek's good fortune, as MB2 Motorsports hired Nemechek to drive the No. 01 U.S. Army car for the balance of the 2003 season and all of 2004 as Nadeau recovered from injuries incurred training for the Richmond race. Nadeau was promised an MB2 ride for 2005, but Nemechek remains confident that his experience and energy will keep him behind a Cup car wheel.

"I'm not a young gun, but I'm not an old-timer. I'm kind of in-between," he said. "There's still a lot of competition left in me."

RYAN NEWMAN

In most cases, the racing dreams of kids growing up in Indiana don't involve stock cars. After all, that's the home of the Indianapolis 500, the very heartbeat of open-wheel racing.

Ryan Newman isn't the typical case. His degree in vehicle structural engineering from Purdue University should tell us that.

"I always wanted to race stock cars," said this native of South Bend. "I always wanted to win the Daytona 500."

Newman hasn't won the sport's most prestigious race yet, but give him time. He seems to accomplish everything he sets his mind to on a racetrack. He's been grabbing poles and winning races ever since he was a youngster.

When SPEED Channel picked Newman as its driver of the year in 2003, it was just the second time in the 37-year history of the award that it didn't go to a series winner. Yet, Newman could well have been Winston Cup champion in 2003 had it not been for a slew of DNFs in the season's first half. In 10 of the season's first 15 races, he did not complete a full race, was ranked 38th or lower in six of them and had a frightening crash in the Daytona 500. In the five he did finish, he had two wins, two fifth-place finishes and a seventh. It was that kind of a Jekyll-and-Hyde year for Newman, who was in just his third full year in NASCAR's showcase series. He finished sixth in points for the second straight year, won a phenomenal eight

NO. 12

BORN: December 8, 1977, South Bend, Ind.

HOBBIES: Fishing, radio-controlled cars

TEAM: Penske Racing

CAR: Dodge

SPONSOR: Mobil1/ALLTEL

CUP WINS: 9

2003 CUP EARNINGS: $6,100,877

CAREER EARNINGS: $11,950,629

The Newman team celebrates with the car (above) and the drinks (opposite) after his Tropicana 400 win in July 2003.

races and took 11 poles, the most by any driver in 23 years. He also had a series-high 17 top-five finishes, and led more miles (1,509.13) than any other driver.

Driving for the Penske Racing South team, Newman is teamed with crew chief Matt Borland, who is also an engineer. "So we're a lot alike in our thinking and our thought process," Newman said.

Newman's parents started him racing in Quarter Midget cars before he was 5 years old, and he eventually became a superstar in Midget racing, all the while excelling at school. In 1993, when he was 15, he was not only All-American Midget Series Rookie of the Year, he won the series championship. An impressive string of

rookie of the year titles would follow: USAC National Midgets in 1995, USAC Silver Crown in 1996 and Sprint cars in 1999.

He was the USAC Coors Light Silver Bullet Series national champion in 1999, with two wins and 12 top-10 finishes in just 15 races. He also won seven times in Midgets. That season helped him reach his dream of a stock car ride, and he made his debut in an ARCA race at Michigan. He won in his next start, at Pocono, and took two more checkered flags in ARCA races that season. In November, Roger Penske gave him his first Cup start at Phoenix, but he ran into engine problems and finished 41st.

The 2001 season was what Newman calls his "ABC" experience. He raced twice in ARCA, 15

In what was a rough start to the 2003 season, Newman rolled his Dodge in a frightening crash at the Daytona 500.

"The attitude was to win races, poles, the rookie title and to finish in the top-10 in points. It was a lot, but we did it."

times in the Busch Series and seven times in the Cup Series. He won Michigan in his ninth Busch start and landed six poles. Newman landed a pole position in his third Cup start, at the Coca-Cola 600, tying Mark Martin's record for earliest pole in a career. He also finished second overall at Kansas.

That busy and varied season set the tone for a quick bolt up the standings in 2002.

"The goal was to utilize what we learned in the ABC program and build on it," Newman said. "The attitude was to win races, poles, the rookie title and to finish in the top-10 in points. It was a lot, but we did it."

Newman set the tone for his breakthrough 2002 season by winning The Winston, the prestigious all-star event, in May. At New Hampshire in September 2002, his 34th career start, Newman won his first Cup race, and he finished sixth in the points race. In an amazingly consistent season, he tied Mark Martin for the most top-10 finishes, with 22, setting a rookie record. He was in the top-five a total of 14 times, one less than series champ Tony Stewart. He also led the Winston Cup Series with six poles, one better than Davey Allison's previous

rookie record. He edged out Jimmie Johnson in one of the most hotly contested Raybestos Rookie of the Year races in years.

"It was unbelievable," Newman said. "I just feel like I have some of the best people you could ask for on my team."

That team switched from Ford to Dodge in 2003, and Newman finished sixth in points again. After the rough start, he went on a 13-race hot streak beginning in July when he won six times, although some wins were dotted with controversy. When he held off Bill Elliott to win the Banquet 400 at Kansas City by going the final 117 miles on one tank of fuel, some drivers accused his team of bending the rules. Newman and his crew chief said their fuel conservation and horsepower were the product of superior Penske Racing engine builders.

"I can tell you first-hand we don't cheat," Newman said. "It's hard when you're criticized for doing well."

For a guy who comes from an open-wheel neighborhood, Ryan Newman has done very, very well.

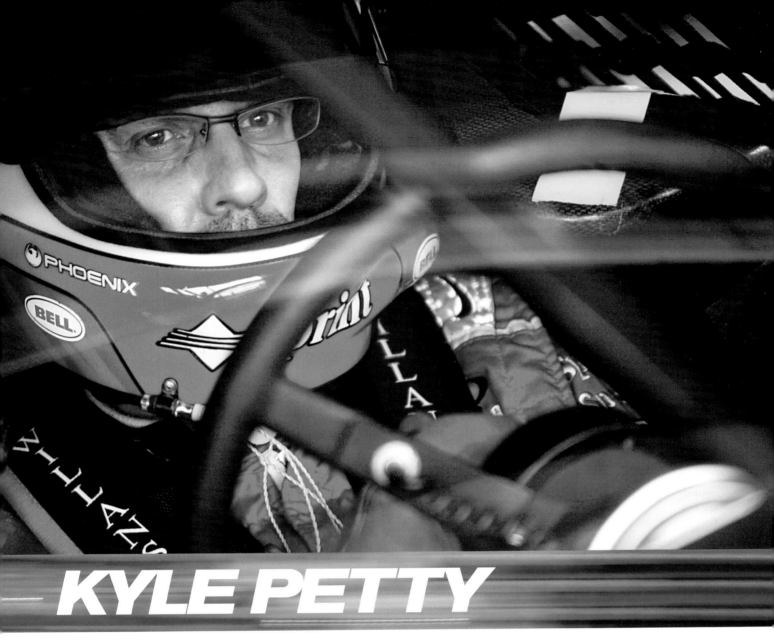

KYLE PETTY

Petty.

The name resonates around stock car tracks like thunder through a canyon. It's the name of the first winner of the Daytona 500, the name of "The King" and the name of a multi-generation family in NASCAR history.

If you're a racer named Petty, the name can be a tailwind when you're winning, but a strong headwind when you're not. Unfortunately in recent years, Kyle Petty hasn't been winning very much.

"When I see a fan sitting in the front row wearing a Kyle Petty T-shirt and I see where we finished in the standings, it was humiliating for me, personally," Petty admitted as he led Petty Enterprises into the 2004 season. "We have to

fix our world before we fix his."

Petty was coming off a 37th-place finish in series points, and was nine years removed from his most recent NASCAR victory. There were widespread rumblings that he would retire from the cockpit and concentrate on running the family racing business, but he vigorously denied those rumors.

Racing fans are always going to talk about Petty. He has grown up under a microscope: the son of Richard Petty, who has twice as many career Cup victories as any other driver in history, and the grandson of Lee Petty, one of NASCAR's charter heroes. Yet he doesn't worry what people think.

"If I did, I wouldn't wear my hair like this," he

NO. 45

BORN: June 20, 1960, Trinity, N.C.

HOBBIES: Riding motorcycles, collecting books

TEAM: Petty Enterprises

CAR: Dodge

SPONSOR: Georgia-Pacific/ Brawny Dodge

CUP WINS: 8

2003 CUP EARNINGS: $2,293,222

CAREER EARNINGS: $17,822,863

Struggling for the past several seasons, Petty will continue the family legacy in his own style. He is the most charity-oriented driver of the NASCAR circuit.

said, laughing and indicating his ponytail, the only such hairstyle in all of NASCAR's three national racing series.

Kyle Petty was raised at tracks and in garages. Less than two months after he was born, he was with his parents at a race in Daytona Beach. Growing up in Level Cross, N.C., he worked in the family garage, got behind the wheel as often as he could, helped in the pit and learned the racing business from every angle.

Still, his life wasn't just about cars, and Petty didn't quite fit the stereotypical stock car driver mold. He was an all-round athlete, offered college scholarships in baseball and in football, where he was a highly-recruited quarterback. He is also talented enough as a musician that

there was talk of a career as a country singer.

However, if you're a Petty, you race stock cars. So, four months before he turned 19, Kyle Petty climbed behind the wheel for the ARCA 200 at Daytona, his first race on a closed circuit. Naturally he won, and later that year his father entered him in five races in NASCAR's premier division. His debut came at Talladega and he was a respectable ninth.

In 1980, he was third in the rookie-of-the-year standings behind Jody Ridley and Lake Speed, and he registered six top-10 finishes. He raced six years for the family firm, usually finishing between 12th and 16th in the drivers' points race, before switching to the Wood Brothers in 1985. It was a tremendous debut as

he moved up to ninth overall, had seven top-fives and was named "Comeback Driver of the Year."

The next season, Petty won the first premier series race of his career, at Richmond, and his family became the first three-generation winners in NASCAR history. After three more years with the Wood Brothers, and one more victory, he joined newcomer Felix Sabates' SABCO team for eight seasons. The first year was forgettable – 30th place, and just two top-10s – but in 1990, Petty jumped up to 11th in series points and enjoyed a dominant victory at Rockingham, where he has traditionally had his best results. Sabates was so elated with the win he gave his driver a Rolls-Royce in appreciation.

Petty had two great seasons for Sabates, finishing fifth in points in both 1992 and 1993. He won six races over their eight-year collaboration, but after finishing 30th and then 27th in the standings, he migrated back to the family-owned business. He started his own team "pe2" and learned about NASCAR life as a car owner. Two years later, he moved pe2 back to Level Cross, and brought it under the Petty Enterprises umbrella. As his father became more of an advisor, Kyle Petty took over much of the day-to-day operation.

Still, after a 15th place finish in 1998, the results weren't there. Petty was 30th in 1998 and 26th in 1999, but all that paled beside the tragedy of May 12, 2000, when Petty's 19-year-old son Adam was killed during a Busch Series race. Devastated, Petty drove only 19 times on the premier series that year. Instead, out of respect for his son, he moved from his No. 44 Winston Cup car to drive Adam's No. 45 in the Busch Series.

Already one of the most charity-oriented drivers in racing history, Petty intensified his efforts after Adam's death. His motorcycle Charity Ride Across America began in 1995 and is the most successful community service event run by a NASCAR driver. He and his wife Pattie have also worked with several other charities, and in 2004 the Victory Junction Gang Camp for children with chronic diseases, dedicated to the memory of their son, Adam, was set to open near Level Cross.

While he struggles to get his No. 45 car – and Petty Enterprises – back to the winner's circle, Kyle Petty knows that giving back to the community is more important. He was named NASCAR's Winston Cup Illustrated Person of the Year in 1999 and 2000 – the only individual to have won in consecutive years.

Petty getting gas and tires at Darlington in March of 2004. He finished 34th.

Petty doesn't worry what people think. "If I did, I wouldn't wear my hair like this."

ELLIOTT SADLER

NO. 38

BORN: April 30, 1975, Emporia, Va.

HOBBIES: Golf, deer hunting, water sports

TEAM: Robert Yates Racing

CAR: Ford

SPONSOR: M&M's

CUP WINS: 2

2003 CUP EARNINGS: $3,795,174

CAREER EARNINGS: $13,184,295

The Robert Yates Racing team had waited a long time to get this checkered flag, but their driver had outwaited them all.

When Elliott Sadler hung on to win at Texas Motor Speedway in April 2004 in his bright No. 38 M&M's Ford, it was as sweet as candy to the RYR team, which hadn't had a win in the 14 months that had passed since Dale Jarrett won at Rockingham.

Sadler himself wondered if his second career win was ever going to happen. The talented young driver had been more than three years without a victory and was taking a pretty strong ribbing from the rest of the driving fraternity. Then, just three weeks before his

29th birthday, he held off Kasey Kahne to win by 0.02 seconds at Texas, the eighth-closest finish in NASCAR's premier series history.

"Some of the guys were picking on me," Sadler said. "They were saying 'You've only won one race!' They were teasing me week in and week out, so to come here and win is very special."

More wins are expected out of Sadler, who's got solid RYR backing and a good sponsor. He was a star in the Busch Series and credits the experience there with helping him win at Texas. After four very average Cup years with the Wood Brothers, and a familiarizing, but ultimately unsuccessful, debut season with Yates in 2003, Sadler said after the Texas win, that "we

feel we really belong now."

He's belonged pretty well anywhere there's been a car, a track and a set of flags. Elliott got behind the wheel of a go-kart at the age of 7 and became so good so quickly that by the time he finished he had won 200 races, several karting championships and the 1983 and 1984 Virginia state titles.

By the time he was 18, he was ready to move into Late Model stocks at the closest track, the South Boston Speedway – the same oval where Jeff Burton had made a big name for himself while Sadler was in his first couple of years in go-karts.

He ran the NASCAR Dodge Weekly Series, and in 1995 took the South Boston track cham-

pionship, winning a phenomenal six straight races on his way to 13 victories for the season. That same year, he ran a limited NASCAR Busch Series schedule for Gary Bechtel's Diamond Ridge Motorsports. He also kept a part-time Busch schedule in 1996, before moving to NASCAR's No. 2 circuit full-time in 1997.

Sadler started his Busch rookie season in fine style, winning the pole at the opening race in Daytona and collecting his first series win at Nazareth, in just his 13th Busch race. He finished fifth in points in 1997 and eighth in 1998, winning five times over the two years.

He was ready to move up, but in the late-1990s there wasn't as much interest in young drivers from owners on the Cup circuit as there

More wins are expected of Sadler, who's got a good sponsor and solid backing in the Robert Yates Ford.

Elliott Sadler had a frustrating 2003 season, as shown here, but has six top-fives halfway through the 2004 season including a win at Texas.

Just three weeks before his 29th birthday, he held off Kasey Kahne to win by 0.02 seconds at Texas, the eighth-closest finish in NASCAR's premier series history.

is today. Sadler had to be content with two 1998 premier series starts for Bechtel.

He got his first big break before the 1999 season when the Wood Brothers released Michael Waltrip. They signed Sadler to a multi-year contract to replace Waltrip as their only Cup series driver.

Sadler finished all but two races that year and was a runner-up to Tony Stewart as rookie of the year. His 24th-place finish in the drivers' standings was acceptable, but he was 20 places back of Stewart and had only one top-10 finish.

It was anticipated that the team would improve in 2000, but Sadler again had only one top-10 finish and slipped to 29th in the standings. Unhappy with the Wood chassis, the team used a Roush chassis in three races.

Things didn't look much better in 2001, especially in March when Sadler wrecked his main car in practice at Bristol and was obliged to start 38th on a provisional in a backup car. Still, he worked his way up toward the front of the pack, and a daring pit call by crew chief Pat Tyson helped Sadler to his first Cup win. It was also the first win for the Wood Brothers in eight years.

Following a pattern of starting well but hitting speed bumps in mid-season, Sadler's DNFs equaled his top-10s (two) that year. He opened strongly again in 2002, finishing second

at the Daytona 500 and at Darlington, but halfway through the season he started to have more misfortunes with his car on the track.

Meanwhile, behind-the-scene negotiations were taking place on two fronts. Ricky Rudd announced that he was getting ready to leave Robert Yates Racing. Sadler began talking to Jack Roush about replacing Rudd, while Rudd was headed, ironically, to the Wood Brothers.

Replacing Rudd at RYR in an all-star lineage that went back to Ernie Irvan and Davey Allison might have been a dream come true, but 2003 was an inconsistent year for Sadler. There were two top-fives, nine top-10s and two poles, but there were also nine DNFs and a frustrating 22nd-place finish in the points standings. With about a dozen races to go, RYR shifted personnel and brought in Todd Parrott as Sadler's crew chief.

"I'm glad we had the 12 or 13 races to work with each other in 2003," Sadler said. "He's a very demanding crew chief, and I didn't know how to take that at first. But as time went on we became better friends and are finishing each other's sentences now."

They're also finishing first.

"To be able to pull into victory lane and see smiling faces is a great, great feeling," Sadler said.

JIMMY SPENCER

Time may have slowed him down just a bit on the track, but it's done nothing to dim Jimmy Spencer's competitive fires.

He is flamboyant and brash, races hard and says what he thinks, no matter what.

"My weakness is probably my temper," Spencer said. "I tend to get a bit emotional."

Spencer, who turned 47 on the day of the 2004 Daytona 500, showed he's as feisty as the youngest pup when his feud with Kurt Busch reached the boiling point at Michigan International Speedway in August 2003. Enraged at Busch, whom he accused of trying to flatten his bumper, Spencer reached into Busch's car in the garage area and punched the younger driver.

Spencer was fined $25,000 by NASCAR, suspended for a week and put on probation for the rest of the season.

Spencer has been known as "Mr. Excitement" since early in his driving career, as he's aggressive on the track and can be seen as a throwback to an earlier era when "rubbing" was an essential part of the sport.

Growing up in Berwick, Pa., Spencer immediately gravitated toward fast cars. His father and brother were both racers, and when Spencer was 15, he crept into the garage area during an Indy-car event at Pocono Raceway and met the legendary A. J. Foyt.

Spencer began racing at Pennsylvania's Port Royal Speedway and moved into Modified cars.

NO. 7

BORN: February 15, 1957, Berwick, Pa.

HOBBIES: Golf, gardening

TEAM: Morgan-McClure Motorsports

CAR: Dodge

SPONSOR: Morgan-McClure

CUP WINS: 2

2003 CUP EARNINGS: $2,565,803

CAREER EARNINGS: $17,449,977

Off the course at Watkins Glen in 2003, Spencer's driving style is a throwback to earlier times.

Opposite: Spencer on the outside at Kansas in 2003 as Kurt Busch drives below him. A driver who says what he thinks, Spencer is a flamboyant figure.

By 1979, he was rookie of the year in the Modified division at the famed Shangri-La Speedway in Oswego, N.Y. He worked his way up the ladder to become a true legend in the Modified division, eventually winning back-to-back NASCAR Featherlite Modified Series championships in 1986 and 1987.

He ran full-time in the Busch Series in 1988, and has competed frequently on that circuit ever since, even entering his own car in later years. After his first full season in Busch, Spencer got a chance to move up to the then Winston Cup Series on a limited schedule for the Baker-Schiff team, making his first start at Bristol in June 1989. He finished 34th without even having a chance to test-drive the car.

"I had wanted to do this my whole life, so when I got the phone call, it was pretty neat," Spencer recalled. "I was nervous. I was running against Richard Petty, Dale Earnhardt, Cale

Yarborough and those guys."

That was the start of Spencer's long run in the premier Cup Series, and also of driving for five different teams in four years. He moved to Rod Osterlund's team in 1990, finishing 24th in series points, then began a long relationship with Travis Carter in 1991, finishing 25th but picking up his first top-five result (third at North Wilkesboro).

In 1992, running a full Busch Series schedule, Spencer also ran a piecemeal premier Cup Series schedule for three different teams. He drove seven times for Carter, four for Bobby Allison and once for Dick Moroso. It was the Allison ride that really did it for Spencer, as his four races produced three top-five finishes and a full-time contract for 1993.

Although he still hadn't won a race in the premier series, 1993 was Spencer's best overall season. He came 12th in the points standings

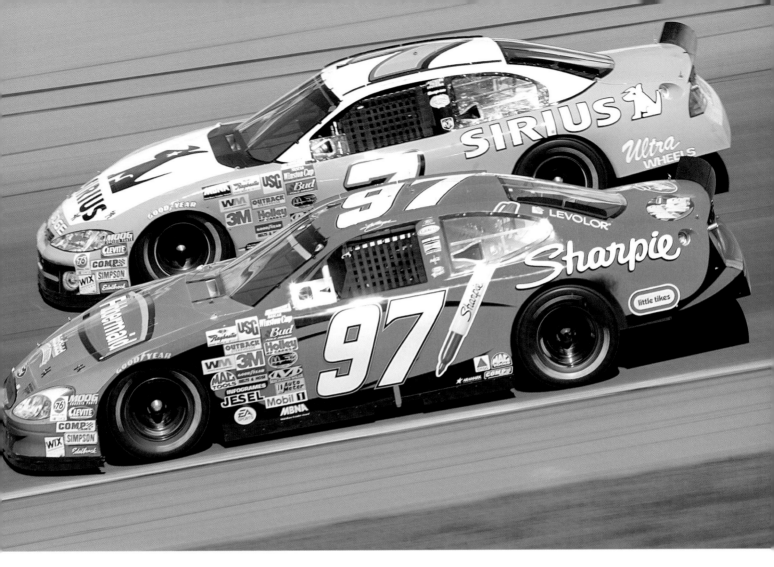

when the team was spending about half as much as those above them. His second at Talladega was his best finish to date and foreshadowed future success on the superspeedways.

"The only thing I do regret about racing for Bobby Allison was that he never got the sponsor he needed," Spencer said.

Spencer moved from one legend to another in 1994, when he left Allison for Junior Johnson. Although he was 29th in the points race because of 11 DNFs, he won his first two races. The final lap of his inaugural victory, at the Pepsi 400 in Daytona, was one of the best in Cup history as he and Ernie Ervan rubbed each other all the way to the flag. He also won at the DieHard 500 at Talladega.

Despite the two wins, Spencer's ride with Johnson survived only one year, and in 1995 he reunited with owner Travis Carter. They stayed together for seven years, although there were no

victories and the best finishes were 14th in 1998 and 15th in 1996. There were, however, second places at Talladega in 1998 and Bristol in 1999. In his final year with Carter in 2001, Spencer won two poles, his first in seven years.

Spencer drove the 2002 season for Chip Ganassi. "But I didn't get along with the people there," he said. So, after a 27th overall finish, he moved to owner Jim Smith's Ultra Motorsports at the start of 2003.

He finished 29th and had four top-10 finishes, but that season will always be remembered for his altercation with Busch. That didn't do much to help his relationship with a certain segment of race fans.

"There are a lot of fans out there who don't like me and I don't really care," Spencer said. "There's a whole lot more who like me and I care about those people."

"My weakness is probably my temper. I tend to get a bit emotional."

TONY STEWART

NO. 20

BORN: May 20, 1971, Rushville, Ind.

HOBBIES: Bowling, pool

TEAM: Joe Gibbs Racing

CAR: Chevrolet

SPONSOR: Home Depot

CUP WINS: 15

2003 CUP EARNINGS:
$5,227,503

CAREER EARNINGS:
$19,254,946

Tony Stewart is one of NASCAR's most charismatic drivers. Before this Indiana native set his sights on driving in the Winston Cup Series, he won three karting titles, four United States Auto Club (USAC) championships and one Indy Racing League (IRL) title. Then in just four years of stock car competition, 32-year-old Stewart won the 2002 NASCAR championship in his Home Depot–sponsored Chevrolet.

"With the caliber of teams, car owners, crew chiefs and drivers that are in Winston Cup, that alone makes you respect this championship," said Stewart after winning the title. "It doesn't take away from any of the other ones I've earned, but this is one that's so pressure-packed

it's an obstacle to itself. That's something I never had with the other championships. This Winston Cup deal is quite a bit different."

Starting with karts at an early age in Indiana, Stewart moved up through the ranks of open-wheeled competition, from Midget to Sprint to Silver Crown cars, winning several USAC titles. He entered the newly formed IRL in 1996 and was named Rookie of the Year in the Indy Racing Northern Light Series. The next year he graduated to the IRL series and won the championship. Stewart then entered the world of full-fendered stock car racing.

After a winless record in NASCAR's Busch Series with the Joe Gibbs Racing and Ranier/Walsh Racing teams, he drove a limited

Winston Cup schedule in 1999 and took a ninth and fourth, respectively, in the Indy 500 and Coca-Cola 600 Winston Cup races. In 2000, Stewart began to show his winning ways, leading the season with six wins and placing sixth in the points standings with 12 top-five and 23 top-10 finishes. In 2001, Stewart placed second in the points standings behind Jeff Gordon, winning three events and taking 15 top-fives and 22 top-10s.

Stewart has always been a fierce competitor, due in part to his father, Nelson. "He never let me settle for second," Stewart said. "He never pressured me to be the best race car driver in the world, but did pressure me to be the best race car driver I could be. He pushed me hard,

but was fair about it. That's probably why you see so much fire in me today."

Stewart won the 2002 NASCAR championship by a mere 38 points, accomplished in the last race of the season. Going into the Talladega race, Stewart took the points lead in October of 2002 with six races left.

"If I had to retype my resume tomorrow, I'd put the Winston Cup championship at No. 1," said Stewart. "All of the championships I've been a part of were hard to acquire. None of them were easy. They had their unique set of circumstances, obstacles and challenges to overcome."

Stewart did not win the 2003 Winston Cup title, as his teams spent most of the off-season

Earning his stripes in the open-wheeled worlds of USAC and IRL, this Indiana native has proven he can win in a car with fenders, capturing the 2002 NASCAR championship.

Stewart's Home Depot Chevy gets the pit treatment at Lowe's Motor Speedway in October 2003.

Opposite: Shaking the champagne at Pocono in June of 2003. The win was the first of two for the year. Stewart placed seventh in the standings.

switching from a Pontiac to a Chevrolet, and it took the team a large part of the 2003 season to make the new car as competitive as possible. Still, the team finished seventh in the standings with two wins, 12 top-five finishes and 18 top-10 finishes in the 36-race schedule. Although he was usually in the running, Stewart's car suffered some engine woes in the early races.

After the longest win drought in his NASCAR career, Stewart finally put the Home Depot Chevy in the winners' circle with a victory in the Pocono 500. It appeared the team's engine woes were now behind them.

Stewart said he thought the team was in good shape when it went to Darlington in March for the Carolina Dodge Dealers 400. "We felt like we were going to have another shot at another title, and then we got off track a little bit through the mid-part of the year. We struggled in some places and we had some terrible luck at other places."

Nevertheless, he got back in form for the next six events, capturing three third-place finishes, a second and a fourth. This streak moved Stewart up four notches in the points standings, and provided a possible chance for his second Winston Cup title with three races left in the schedule. After qualifying sixth in the Checker

Auto Parts 500 at Phoenix, however, he placed a dismal 18th. A ninth-place finish in the Pop Secret 400 at Rockingham and a season-ending seventh finish in the Ford 400 at Homestead-Miami Speedway wasn't enough for Stewart to retain his title.

Going into the 2004 season, Stewart retained his relationship with Joe Gibbs Racing and Home Depot. He has signed on with the team through 2009.

During his short NASCAR career, Stewart's off-track temper has gotten the better of him. Twice in 2002, Stewart had altercations with photographers. In August, he was fined $10,000 and the Home Depot team was fined $50,000 after Stewart shoved a photographer at the Indy race. Another incident occurred at the season-ending Homestead race of 2002, but Stewart's apology was accepted.

Since that time, Stewart has become one of the sport's best ambassadors, and his off-track demeanor has risen to the level of professionalism he applies on the race track.

RUSTY WALLACE

NO. 2

BORN: August 14, 1956, St. Louis, Mo.

HOBBIES: Flying, golf

TEAM: Penske Racing

CAR: Dodge

SPONSOR: Miller Lite

CUP WINS: 55

2003 CUP EARNINGS: $3,766,740

CAREER EARNINGS: Over $39 million

At 47 years of age, the racing world was starting to think Rusty Wallace was just taking up a spot on the track. It was time for the veteran to retire and leave the glory and the driving to the "young guns."

Then the former NASCAR Cup champion proved the desire is still strong when he won the Advance Auto Parts 500 at Martinsville in April 2004. It was Wallace's first Cup win in 105 races – his first victory in three years.

"I questioned a lot of things for a long time during that dry spell," Wallace said after the Martinsville win. "It feels good to finally get back in victory lane."

With this win, Wallace now has 55 Cup victories to his credit, and passed Lee Petty for sixth

on the all-time win list. "It's an honor to be compared to those guys, such as Petty, Allison, or Pearson. They were tough cats."

A native of St. Louis, Mo., Wallace spearheaded the trend to non-Southern U.S. drivers to make their mark in NASCAR racing. He ran his first Cup race in 1980 and competed full-time starting in 1984 with the Cliff Stewart Racing Team. For the next four years, he drove for the Blue Max Racing Team, and since 1991 has been driving the familiar No. 2 for Roger Penske.

Wallace began racing in 1973, won many short-track events in the 1970s and then toured with USAC's stock car circuit in 1979. He won five races in his first year with USAC and

placed second in points.

He then raced in the ASA Late Model Series, becoming a standout in that Midwest-U.S. series and taking the championship in 1983.

Aside from a strong passion to drive, Wallace became very adapt at "reading" a car on the track and developed into an excellent chassis tuner. He took this knowledge to Cup racing where he was able to contribute to the handling of a race car in NASCAR's premier series.

In 1986, Wallace won his first Cup race, the Valleydale 500 at Bristol. Two years later he captured six wins and placed second in the standings. He also won six races in his championship year of 1989, highlighted by winning the Winston All-Star event. His 20 top-10 finishes

in 29 races allowed him to win the title over Dale Earnhardt by just 12 points. He captured a career season-best of 10 races in 1993, but placed second to Earnhardt.

With his 14th-place standings in 2003, Wallace finished in the top 20 in points for 20 consecutive seasons, the longest current active streak. And he has no intention of slowing down.

"I'm not a quitter," he said. "I've never quit. If anything I just keep moving things around to complement what I've got."

Wallace is a second-generation driver. His father, Russ, was a strong competitor on the tracks of Missouri. Rusty, along with brothers Kenny and Mike, caught the racing bug as

Wallace makes a hasty exit from his burning car. He is a veteran on the NASCAR circuit, teaming up with Penske in 1991.

A sweet victory for Wallace at Martinsville in 2004, his first in three years. "It feels good to finally get back in victory lane." This win made him sixth on the all-time NASCAR win list.

Right: Wallace leads Ward Burton on his way to a Martinsville win.

"I'm not a quitter. I've never quit. If anything I just keep moving things around to complement what I've got."

young men, and all three continue to compete to this day. Wallace has said his heroes are his father and NASCAR legend Bobby Allison.

Aside from his passion for racing, Wallace also has a passion for flying, which started as a sideline to his racing in 1981.

Back in the early 1980s, Wallace was spreading himself thin trying to get to all the races and had a friend fly him to his various ASA and All-Pro shows around the country. He envied Bobby Allison at that time, as he would fly in to a short-track race, get in a car and run for a few hours, and then fly back out.

By 1984 Wallace got his pilot's license, and has since maintained a strong interest in flying. His Diamond Aviation company is comprised of several aircraft, including Lear jets and a Bell helicopter. Wallace himself now has his jet pilot's license, and has accumulated about 10,000 hours of flight time.

Even after his Martinsville win, Wallace will continue to fly around to the tracks in his 24th year of Cup racing. He believes he has built a strong team for 2004 with his Miller Lite Dodge, and all members are now working in harmony. He said he hasn't changed his approach to driving, but he has changed his approach and methods to getting a competitive car on the track.

"I don't feel I'm driving any different," he said, "but we've applied different technical set-ups on the car. We've been there, but we've just had bad pit stops for over a year." He now has more confidence in facing the "young guns," demonstrating he still can win.

"This is the best I've felt in a long time."

MICHAEL WALTRIP

A few years ago, Michael Waltrip took up marathon running. It probably helped that he already knew how long it can take to reach an important goal.

In 2001, when Waltrip won the big daddy of all stock car races – the Daytona 500 – it snapped his record 462 Cup starts without a checkered flag.

Even though he won the 500 again in 2003, Waltrip still had trouble gaining respect from a certain segment of racing fans. He went from being the guy who was only racing because of his famous brother to the guy who could only win restrictor-plate races. That his only two other premier series victories have come at Talladega, another restrictor-plate track, fueled that mostly unfair criticism.

"I just don't pay attention when people say stuff like that," Waltrip said. "I've won 10 Busch races and never at a plate race. They've all come at tracks like Darlington, Charlotte and Bristol.

"But I really feel that when I start those restrictor-plate races, I know everything I need to know in order to win."

All of Waltrip's big victories have come since he caught a huge career break in late 2000 when Dale Earnhardt asked him to drive DEI's third car. Although Earnhardt died soon thereafter – in the very Daytona 500 which vindicated his trust in his new driver – and Waltrip had some struggles later that first season, he secured his place by signing a driving contract with DEI

NO. 15

BORN: **April 30, 1963, Owensboro, Ky.**

HOBBIES: **Distance running, golf, tennis**

TEAM: **Dale Earnhardt Inc.**

CAR: **Chevrolet**

SPONSOR: **NAPA Auto Parts**

CUP WINS: **4**

2003 CUP EARNINGS: **$4,929,620**

CAREER EARNINGS: **$22,945,465**

Two-time Daytona 500 winner Waltrip (No. 15) didn't get to finish the Sharpie 500 at Bristol in 2003 after smacking up with Rusty Wallace (No. 2).

which lasts through 2006.

Waltrip said of the late Earnhardt gambling on a winless veteran driver: "I think he thought, 'You have talent as a driver but you haven't done a good job so far. I'm going to straighten this deal out for you.'"

Loaded with southern charm, Waltrip is one of the most engaging men in Cup racing. He is 16 years younger than his famous brother Darrell (who won NASCAR's premier series points title three times), but Michael Waltrip didn't start racing until the relatively advanced age of 12 when he bought a go-kart. He laughs over the fact that his parents, tired out by all the time they'd put into Darrell's early career, wouldn't even let him keep the car at home.

"I've never considered myself just Darrell's brother," Waltrip said. "I've never raced a car wanting to be better than Darrell. I've always just raced because that's what I've wanted to do. But when I was a kid growing up in Kentucky, no one else's brother was off racing against Richard Petty."

He admits that the Waltrip name and Darrell's input helped him land some sponsorships early in his career.

Waltrip won his first competitive race in go-karts at 12, and after a successful run he moved to stock cars in 1981, the same year Darrell won the first of back-to-back Winston Cup points titles. He won on his first day in stocks, too, setting the track record in the Mini-Modified

Division at Kentucky Motor Speedway, then going on to win the division title that season.

In 1983, at the age of 20, he won NASCAR's Goody Dash Series championships and was voted the series' most popular driver two straight years. He moved to North Carolina from Kentucky and lived with Richard and Lynda Petty for a while, soaking up driving knowledge from "The King."

Waltrip got his first Cup Series ride, for Richard Bahre, at Charlotte in May 1985. His brother won the race. The younger Waltrip was 28th and went on to race four more times on the premier circuit before signing a full-time contract with Bahre the next year. He was 19th in series points in 1986, finishing second to Alan Kulwicki in the rookie standings.

"When I first came in, we competed with used engines and used tires and used cars and we had no hope for a win," Waltrip said. "We just wanted to survive."

From 1988 to 1995, Waltrip raced for Chuck Rider, picking up a second place finish (Pocono) in his first season on the team. Although he finished 12th in points standings in the final two years with Rider, he didn't win and had only 15 top-five finishes.

He moved on to the Wood Brothers in 1996 and got off to an encouraging first year with a victory in The Winston, an all-star event, but he had only one top-five in three years with the Woods. In 1998, he failed to qualify at Phoenix, the first time he'd missed the cut in 387 straight starts.

In 1999, he joined Mattei Motorsports and finished fifth in the Daytona 500, but after 19 races in 2000, he finished the year in a Jim Smith car.

That's when Dale Earnhardt entered the picture.

"When Dale put Michael in that car, that's what Michael needed – not necessarily that car but that confidence," Darrell Waltrip said. His brother agreed. He felt it was the first time he'd really had a chance to win races.

"I did doubt myself a bit, but I wasn't a strong enough person to change my position and make it the right situation for me," Michael Waltrip said. "Now – shoot, I'm happy."

Who wouldn't be happy winning two Daytona 500s and two Talladegas within three years. It didn't silence all the critics, but it muffled quite a few.

"Winning Daytona didn't change the way I looked at myself so much," Waltrip said, "but it sure changed the way other people looked at me."

Waltrip's big break came in 2000 when he was asked by Dale Earnhardt to drive the DEI team's third car, a far cry from his early years. "When I first came in, we competed with used engines and used tires and used cars and we had no hope for a win."

"I've never raced a car wanting to be better than Darrell. I've always just raced because that's what I've wanted to do."

BRENDAN GAUGHAN

NO. 77

BORN: July 10, 1975, Las Vegas, Nev.

HOBBIES: Off-roading, basketball

TEAM: Penske-Jasper Racing

CAR: Dodge

SPONSOR: Kodak

- When Roger Penske signed him for the 2004 season, it made Gaughan the first driver since Dodge's return to NASCAR to move up to Cup racing after driving a factory Dodge in another series.

- He made his Cup debut at the Daytona 500 in 2004 and finished 19th.

- In 2003, he won six Craftsman races – more than anyone else – but an accident with 33 laps remaining in the season relegated him to fourth place in the points standings.

- His four straight wins at Texas Motor Speedway is a Craftsman Truck Series record.

- Gaughan was the 2002 rookie of the year in NASCAR's Craftsman Truck Series.

- Gaughan was once an instructor for the Richard Petty Driving experience at his home track in Las Vegas, Nev.

JAMIE MCMURRAY

NO. 42

BORN: June 3, 1976, Joplin, Mo.

HOBBY: Radio-controlled cars

TEAM: Chip Ganassi Racing

CAR: Dodge

SPONSOR: Texaco/Havoline

- McMurray placed 13th in the 2003 Cup Series – enough to beat Greg Biffle for rookie of the year.

- On October 13, 2002, at Lowe's Motor Speedway, McMurray held off a charging Bobby Labonte on the final lap to win his first NASCAR Premier Series event.

- The win at Lowe's was just the second Cup ride for McMurray and established a modern-era record for fewest starts required for a victory.

- McMurray had more than a dozen top-10 finishes in three years of Busch Series racing.

- He worked his way up to NASCAR's Dodge Weekly Series on Missouri tracks, winning the track championship at I-44 Speedway in 1997.

BRIAN VICKERS

- He began his first full Cup season in 2004.

- Starting in just five Cup races in 2003, mostly for experience, he qualified in the top-five four times, including outside poles at Phoenix and Rockingham.

- He didn't turn 20 years old until near the end of the 2003 season, but he won the Busch points championship with three victories and 13 top-fives.

- In 2002, Vickers qualified for a Busch Series race on Friday, hurried home for his high school graduation, then returned to Charlotte in time for Saturday's race.

- Vickers debuted in NASCAR's Busch Series at the Milwaukee Mile in 2000, when he was just 16.

- Vickers earned rookie of the year honors in the USAR Hooter's Pro-Cup in 2000.

NO. 25

BORN: October 24, 1983, Thomasville, N.C.

HOBBIES: Video games, reading

TEAM: Hendrick Motorsports

CAR: Chevrolet

SPONSOR: GMAC Financial Services

SCOTT WIMMER

- Wimmer turned in a stunning third-place finish at the 2004 Daytona 500.

- He had a ninth-place finish at Phoenix after replacing Ward Burton in the No. 22 Dodge for the final four Cup races of the 2003 season.

- He won four Busch races and finished third in the points championship in 2002, and was runner-up to Greg Biffle for the 2001 series' rookie of the year award.

- In 1994, Wimmer was rookie of the year in three separate series: at State Park Speedway, Dells Motor Speedway and in the Wisconsin Short Track Series.

- He has experience as a crew chief, mechanic and fabricator.

NO. 22

BORN: January 26, 1976, Wausau, Wis.

HOBBIES: Hunting, fishing, skiing

TEAM: Bill Davis Racing

CAR: Dodge

SPONSOR: Caterpillar

LEGENDS

BOBBY ALLISON

BORN: December 3, 1937, Miami, Fla.

CARS DRIVEN: Mercury, Chevrolet, Buick, AMC

YEARS IN CUP RACING: 28 (1961–1988)

CUP WINS: 85

CAREER EARNINGS: $7,673,808

Bobby Allison had one of the most turbulent careers in NASCAR. In his 26 years of Cup racing he also had one of the most successful NASCAR careers.

Starting in 1961, until his retirement in 1998, Allison recorded 85 victories, third on the all-time win list. During those years he finished the season in the top-10 a total of 17 times with five second-place finishes and a NASCAR championship in 1983.

His reputation as one of NASCAR's fiercest competitors started as soon as he got into the top division, when he placed 20th in Ralph Stark's Chevrolet at the 1961 Daytona 500. Even with less than optimum equipment, Allison went up against the best of drivers during his

career and, once established, drove with a presence rarely found in today's racing.

Born in Florida in December 1937, Robert Arthur Allison convinced his mother to sign for him so he could run an old coupe at Hialeah Speedway in 1955. A couple of years after that Allison and his brother Donnie ran the NASCAR Modified races whenever they could afford to.

With a taste for Cup racing in 1961 but no money to run the series, Allison concentrated on his Modified driving, winning this division title three years in a row, from 1962 to 1964. With these credentials and a move to the more stock car–oriented atmosphere around Huey-town, Ala., Allison managed to run eight Grand

National (now Nextel Cup) races for 1965.

He ran 33 races the next year, but funds were tight. He wanted to continue, and with Donnie's help he built a Chevelle at his modest shop for the 1966 season. With this Chevelle, Allison was on his way, winning his first race at Oxford, Me., and two more NASCAR events to finish a respectable 10th in the season.

He raced in 45 events in 1967, for Bud Moore, Cotton Owens and himself, but took two wins when he hooked up with the famed Holman-Moody team. After capturing 11 wins for Holman-Moody in 1971, Allison went to drive for Junior Johnson, picking up another 10 wins in 1972.

Over the next several years, Allison drove for several teams, including Penske and DiGard Racing. It was with the DiGard Buick and a Robert Yates engine that he won the NASCAR Winston Cup title in 1983.

Known as one of the founding members of "The Alabama Gang," Allison received national attention in 1979 during his race-ending fight with Cale Yarborough on the first live telecast of the Daytona 500. His brother Donnie had been leading the race with a lap left, and a determined Yarborough was right behind him. Entering the final turn the cars collided, ending up on the infield grass while Richard Petty cruised to the win.

While this action was taking place, Bobby Allison decided to stop and check on his brother, and after some verbal sparring, the three drivers were physically discussing their views with their fists on television.

Aside from this notoriety, or perhaps because of it, Allison was voted NASCAR's most popular driver six times. He was also bestowed NASCAR's "Award of Excellence" in 1989 and named as one of its "50 Greatest Drivers."

To show he was not just a good ol' stock car boy, he competed in SCCA Trans-Am racing and drove in two Indianapolis 500 events. He started 12th in the 1973 Indy 500, placing 32nd after throwing a rod in the early stages, and he returned in 1975, starting 15th and finishing 25th, out with a broken transmission. He drove for Penske in both Indy races.

Left: Allison would stray from NASCAR competition. Here he is celebrating after winning USAC's Texas 250 in 1979 in his AMC Matador.

Opposite: Allison winning his second Daytona 500 in 1982. He also won the Big One in 1978 and 1988.

Allison also made more "star appearances" during his career than any other Cup driver, flying into oval tracks all over North America as a guest driver, and quite often winning before flying back out the same night.

In 1998, Allison was involved in a career-ending crash. Racing at Pocono, the accident left him with a broken shoulder, left leg, ribs and a brain injury. His recovery was slow but steady, and he turned his racing efforts to helping sons Clifford and Davey.

In 1992, Clifford was killed in a crash at Michigan, and Davey, a successful Cup driver for nine years, was killed in a helicopter accident at Talladega in 1993.

Along with dealing with the loss of his two sons, close friend Neil Bonnett was killed racing in February 1994. Allison struggled to operate his own NASCAR Cup team but called it a day in 1997.

Allison is an accomplished pilot, starting his flying in 1967. He has owned and flown a succession of Aerostar aircraft over the years. He is also a mechanical inventor of some note, developing racing engines and parts for NASCAR competition as well as aircraft engine and propeller items.

He was one of the most competitive individuals in racing. Big track, short track, road course, paved or dirt, Allison was perhaps the toughest racer to beat.

DALE EARNHARDT

BORN: April 29, 1951, Kannapolis, N.C.

CAR DRIVEN: Chevrolet

YEARS IN CUP RACING: 26 (1975–2001)

CUP WINS: 76

CAREER EARNINGS: Over $41 million

Above: No. 3 – The most famous image of NASCAR's modern era.

With a tenacity seldom found in any professional sport, Dale Earnhardt propelled his way into the conscious of the racing public. Through his determination, he became a national symbol, a seven-time NASCAR Cup champion and his name was synonymous with stock car racing.

His racing death at the end of the 2001 Daytona 500 elevated his status to a unprecedented level. To many in countries outside the United States he had represented the American dream.

Earnhardt brought more fans to NASCAR than any other driver. He was known as "The Man in Black" and "The Intimidator" for his unmatched win-at-all-costs attitude. This attitude, along with large amounts of sheer grit, thrust this Kannapolis, N.C., native and Grade 9 dropout to not only the top of NASCAR, but head of his own multi-million-dollar business. His tireless work ethic turned into the most dominant career in NASCAR history.

His racing spanned more than two decades. It included running in 676 races – and winning 76 of these. He took 281 top-five and 428 top-10 finishes. He is also the only six-time winner of the Busch Clash and the only three-time winner of the Winston All-Star race.

Earnhardt was born in 1951, and he developed a passion for stock car racing early on through his father Ralph, a racer of some note throughout the Southeastern United States. While in his teens, Earnhardt worked on his own race cars, starting with hobby-class cars, eking out a racing program that depended on winning to pay back his creditors.

When father Ralph died in 1973, Earnhardt became more determined than ever to be a successful driver. He built cars and raced on the Sportsman circuits at such speedways as Hickory and Concord.

His first Cup ride was in the World 600 at Charlotte in 1975. He drove Ed Negre's Dodge and placed 22nd, winning $2,425. Between 1976 and 1978 he competed in eight events with limited success, but in 1979 dramatic changes were about to occur.

When Dave Marcis left car owner Rod Osterlund, the car owner put Earnhardt behind the wheel – the break Earnhardt considered the biggest in his racing career. In his first full season of Winston Cup (currently Nextel Cup) racing, he took his first victory, a win at Bristol in only his 16th Cup start. He finished the season with 11 top-five finishes, placed seventh in the standings and won rookie-of-the-year honors.

Everything came together – and quickly – in 1980, as Earnhardt won the Cup title with five wins that year. Well into the 1981 season, he drove for the well-established Bud Moore team and took a pair of races in Moore's Fords over the next two years.

Meanwhile, new team owner Richard Childress was starting to build a strong team, and Earnhardt got into the driver's seat starting in 1984. Little did either know what was to happen in the next few seasons.

This team effort took the driver and owner to a level of performance neither imagined, and by 1987, they had captured two Cup championships. Throughout the 1990s, the black No. 3 Chevy became a familiar sight in victory lane, and Earnhardt drove to Cup titles in 1990, 1991, 1993 and 1994. He was a force to be reckoned with and competed with a fierceness and intensity like no other on the circuit. He performed feats few thought possible, always pushing himself and his car for success.

He was often referred to as "The Master of the Draft" for his ability to use this aerodynamic force to win on superspeedways such as Talladega. Even when he developed his own racing team, Dale Earnhardt Incorporated, he continued with his nothing-ventured, nothing-gained mentality, and his status in the racing world continued to climb.

The fire that burned in him as a race car driver also burned Earnhardt off-track. He broke new ground in the NASCAR world through the marketing of himself and his image. His financial successes became just as strong and positive as his racing. His attitude was endearing, and a shining example of triumph over adversity. He drove to win, no matter the circumstances.

Perhaps the best example of his persona came after he was involved in a bad crash in 1996 at Talladega. He severely injured his collarbone, so much so he couldn't finish driv-

ing in the Brickyard 400 at Indy a week after his crash. It was the first time since 1979 Earnhardt could not finish a race due to an injury.

Nevertheless, two weeks after the Talladega incident, Earnhardt – in complete hard-core character, still racked with pain – pushed himself to another level, winning pole position at the Watkins Glen road course event and placing sixth at the end of the race.

Dale Earnhardt was no quitter.

That was the essence in the career of what many consider the greatest stock car driver ever.

Top: Dale Earnhardt in a familiar pose, waving after a victory. This was after his Busch Classic win at Daytona in 1986.

Above: Fellow driver Tim Richmond helps Earnhardt after an ugly crash at Pocono in 1982.

THE FLOCKS

Tim Flock

BORN: May 11, 1924,
Fort Payne, Ala.

CARS DRIVEN: Hudson,
Oldsmobile, Chrysler

YEARS IN CUP RACING: 23
(1949–1961)

CUP WINS: 39

CAREER EARNINGS:
$109,656

*The most prominent
of the Flock family,
Tim Flock (left) raced
Hudsons, Oldsmobile
and Chryslers from
1949 until 1966.
Here he is (right),
congratulated after a
1957 Grand National
victory, one of 40 such
wins of his career. He
won 18 races in 1955
alone.*

*In NASCAR's early years, there were
a lot of charismatic drivers, but the
Flock family retains a special place in
the early history of the sport.*

The Flock family consisted of four brothers
and two sisters, and the family moved to the
Atlanta area from their Alabama home for
better employment opportunities during the
years before World War II.

Brothers Tim, Fonty and Bob learned their
driving skills hauling moonshine around the
back roads of Georgia. Carl raced boats. Sister
Ethel, who also made her mark in racing in
those early years with over 100 races to her
credit, was named after the high-test gasoline of
the time. The youngest Flock, Reo, was named
after the car, and she took to skydiving and
wing-walking.

Born in 1924, Tim Flock started his professional racing career in 1947, running in a
Modified race in North Wilkesboro, N.C. It was
Tim that would have the most successful racing
career in the family, and he was on his way
when he placed fifth at Charlotte in 1949 in
NASCAR's new "Strictly Stock" division, a forerunner of today's Nextel Cup.

He was driving an Olds 88, one of the hottest
cars at the time. Older brother Fonty took
second in the race, driving one of the "Step-
Down" Hudsons. The following year, Tim won
his first NASCAR race, winning the Grand
National event at Charlotte.

For the next several years, Tim Flock became
a dominant force in Grand National racing. He
won his first championship in 1952 behind the
wheel of Ted Chester's Hudson, taking eight
NASCAR events and finishing 14 times in the
top-five.

After an altercation with NASCAR in 1954
over some engine modifications, resulting in
then-president Bill France taking away his
victory, Bill Flock said he would not race
NASCAR again. So he opened up a Pure Oil
station in Atlanta and seemed content with his
new life. Then in 1955, friends convinced him
to travel to Daytona. Remarking out loud he
could win the Daytona race if he had one of the
new Chrysler 300s tearing down the sand
during the beach trials, Flock found himself
introduced to Carl Kiekhaefer, the man behind
the Chrysler assault on NASCAR.

The Mercury Outboard Motor President

needed another driver for his team. Flock got into one of the big Hemi-powered Chryslers and took the pole for the Daytona Beach race. He placed second in the race behind Fireball Roberts, but Roberts' car was deemed illegal, so Flock was on his way. In 1955, he won 18 of his 39 Grand National races and his second NASCAR championship. His 1955 winning season was a NASCAR record that was not broken until Richard Petty won 19 races in 1967.

Tim Flock ran with Kiekhaefer and the Chryslers in 1956, with three wins in his first eight races. However, the spirited Flock was tired of the strict regimentation of Kiekhaefer and quit the team.

He continued to race but never with the same amount of success. In 1961, he ran afoul of Bill France when he attempted to organize a drivers' union with fellow driver Curtis Turner, and both drivers were banned from NASCAR.

Although the ban was lifted in 1966, Tim had soured on driving. He did stay in racing, though, working as program director at the Charlotte Motor Speedway.

Inducted into the International Motorsports Press Hall of Fame in 1991 and the Stock Car Hall of Fame in 1995, Tim Flock died in 1998. He had won 40 races and 37 pole positions in his 13-year NASCAR career. With the 40 victories in 189 starts, Tim Flock holds a winning percentage of 21.2, the best in NASCAR Grand National/Cup history. He also won NASCAR's only sports car race, in 1955, driving a Mercedes-Benz 300 SL Gullwing.

Older brother Fonty did not have as successful a career as Tim, but he was a force to reckon with in NASCAR's early days. Running in semi-organized events prior to World War II, Fonty did well, but he was severely injured in a crash at Daytona in 1941, and he didn't return to racing until 1947.

In May of that year, he won the inaugural stock car race at North Wilkesboro, and continued with victories at Charlotte, Trenton and Greensboro, winning the National Championship Stock Car Circuit, the name used before NASCAR.

Tim's older brother Fonty shown at Daytona Beach with one of the killer Chrysler 300 cars of 1955–56. NASCAR's 1949 Modified champ, Fonty stopped racing in 1957.

In 1949, Fonty won NASCAR's Modified title with 11 victories, and then took to Grand National racing, finishing second in 1951, fourth in 1952, and fifth in 1953. He drove a limited schedule starting in 1954, and after a crash at Darlington in 1957, he parked it for good.

Sister Ethel was not just a flash in the pan racer. Driving brother Fonty's Modified in the late 1940s, she raced in more than 100 events. Although she usually limited her racing to the Atlanta area, she did make a trip to Daytona in July 1949 and drove her Cadillac to an 11th-place finish in a field of 26 competitors, ahead of brothers Fonty and Bob. She also finished ahead of such early notables as Herb Thomas, Curtis Turner and Buck Baker.

DAVID PEARSON

BORN: December 22, 1934, Whitney, S.C.

CARS DRIVEN: Dodge, Ford, Mercury

YEARS IN CUP RACING: 27 (1960–1986)

CUP WINS: 105

CAREER EARNINGS: $2,836,224

Clockwise from top left: David Pearson, shown with the 1976 Southern 500 trophy. Earlier that year, he cajoled his battered Mercury to a win at the Daytona 500. Pearson, the Wood Brothers and the Mercury after the Firecracker 400 win at Daytona in 1972. Pearson celebrates.

One of the great stock car drivers, David Pearson amassed 105 NASCAR Cup victories, second only to all-time leader Richard Petty with 200 wins.

There were times during his 27-year career where his star shone bright. Many speculate that if Pearson had raced as long as Petty he would have taken the title as "The King of Stock Car Racing."

This South Carolina native, born in 1934, was NASCAR champ three times and leads the all-time win ration with 18 percent. As a sample of his strength, Pearson entered only 18 races in 1973 but won 11 of these events.

Pearson started his racing career in 1952 on the dirt tracks near his home. By 1960, he was on the NASCAR circuit, and he took 18th at Daytona that year. The next year he won his first Grand National race (the forerunner of today's Nextel Cup), the World 600, plus the Firecracker 250 and the Dixie 400 at Atlanta, and was the first driver to accomplish this in a single year. He won the 1961 rookie-of-the-year honors with his Chevy, and his reputation was on its way.

Throughout the 1960s. Pearson was a domi-

nant racer in NASCAR's top class, first running in Dodges, and then switching over to the familiar No. 21 Mercury and Ford Talladega mounts.

Pearson's physical attributes played a large part in his success. He was stout in stature, and those days it took a lot of muscle to handle a car in a long race when there was no power steering.

In 1964, he won eight events on the short tracks, and two years later won 10 of 15 races on dirt tracks and enough events on the remainder of the circuit to give him his first NASCAR championship.

By the end of the decade, Pearson's late-race hold-nothing-back, pedal-to-the-floor style had taken hold, and in both 1968 and 1969 he won top honors again.

In 1968, he drove his Ford to 16 wins, and in 1969, he took 11 wins. In those two years he also led 37 and 39 races, respectively. He was the first to break the 190 mile-per-hour barrier at Daytona, qualifying his Ford at 190.029 miles per hour in 1969.

Pearson acquired the nickname "The Silver Fox" for his driving prowess. He was a master at playing his cards close to the vest, never showing what he was capable of until the closing laps of a race. When he was running well, he would lurk back a few positions from the leader, and then near the end would turn it up a few notches to get in the lead on the last lap.

During this heady time in NASCAR history, the rivalry between Pearson and Petty elevated the sport's awareness. Their late-race duels became a mainstay at many a track, and were always exciting, offering some of the most memorable finishes in NASCAR racing. This duo finished one-two 63 times, Pearson taking 33 victories and Petty 30.

One of this pair's most famous finishes occurred at the end of the 1976 Daytona 500, a race Pearson had never won in 17 attempts. As Pearson and Petty entered the last lap on the 2.5-mile oval, Petty led, and all waited for Pearson to make his move. Going into turn three Pearson took the lead, but drifted high near the wall in doing so, and Petty regained the lead, but by only a couple of feet. The two tangled in turn four, with Pearson going into the wall and Petty sliding down into the infield. "The King" was 50 yards away from winning – 50 yards away from the start/finish line with a car he couldn't get started.

With no other cars on the lead lap, Pearson managed to keep the engine running in his Mercury, collected the battered car back up, and limped across the line to win his first Daytona 500.

Pearson did win races after his Daytona victory, but the glory days were gone. He had a couple of wins in 1979 and 1980, winning his last Cup event at Darlington, a treacherous track he was able to master.

Although he never suffered any race-related injuries during his career, Pearson's eyesight was not as good as it once was and, coupled with persistent back problems, he retired from driving in 1986 at age 52.

RICHARD PETTY

BORN: July 2, 1937, Level Cross, N.C.

CARS DRIVEN: Plymouth, Pontiac

YEARS IN CUP RACING: 35 (1958–1992)

CUP WINS: 200

CAREER EARNINGS: $8,541,218

Above, left: A true American icon, Richard Petty celebrates his 200th win at Daytona, the Firecracker 400, in 1984. Above, right: Although it's a Pontiac and not a Plymouth, it's still the No. 43 car, it's still adorned with STP logos and it's still Petty blue. This is the King's Rockingham ride during his final year.

When one thinks of stock car racing, one cannot help but think of Richard Petty. To many fans, he is stock car racing.

During his 34-year racing career, this lanky, dark-haired North Carolina native epitomized stock car racing, and became not only the sport's most famous figure, but one of the most famous personalities in all sports. He has been treated as a hero in many ways. His status with his fans is akin to Elvis Presley, and Petty has truly become "The King" of his sport.

Over his three decades of racing, Petty has deservedly earned his crown, both on and off the track. Not only did he amass a track record that may never be equaled, he did it in his characteristic humble style, never forgetting his fans. With his trademark cowboy boots and hat, Petty always took time at races to sign autographs and chat with people. He always said if it wasn't for the fans, he would not have had such a long and illustrious career.

Nevertheless, his driving skills played an important role in his racing, from the dirt bull-rings in his early years to the superspeedways before he hung up his hat. He not only witnessed, but was a major part of NASCAR's growth and traditions as it established itself from a small regional series to a major nationally conscious sport. Just some of his accomplishments include:

- Most Cup wins, with 200
- Most laps led, with 52,194
- Most races led, with 599
- Most consecutive races won, with 10 in 1967
- Most wins in one season, with 27 in 1967

Born in Level Cross, N.C., in July 1937, Petty grew up in a racing environment. His father, Lee Petty, was one of the stars during NASCAR's first decade, twice winning the Grand National (today's equivalent of the Nextel Cup) title, and winning the first Daytona 500 in 1959.

The Pettys were a family-oriented family, and all members not only went to all the races as a group, they all helped with the operation. Richard and brother Maurice crewed for their father, and Mother Elizabeth scored for the team.

Soon it was Richard's turn to race a car.

"My daddy was a race driver, so I became a race driver," Petty said. "If he'd been a grocer, I might have been a grocer. If he'd been a baseball player, I'd probably have wanted to be a baseball player. But he was a race driver, so here I am. I grew up around race cars. I been working on 'em since I was 12 years old and driving 'em since I was 21. It's all I know, really."

Just after his 21st birthday, Petty entered his first NASCAR race, driving an Oldsmobile in NASCAR's Convertible Class. He finished sixth in that 200-lapper on the old Columbia, S.C., dirt oval. His first win came a year later, in 1959, at the same track. He was on his way.

In 1960, Petty won his first Grand National race, and two years later he finished second in points in NASCAR's top division. In 1963, he captured 14 wins, then in 1964, he won his first of seven Daytona 500 races and also won the division championship.

He then left NASCAR to drag race – yes, drag race – just as his stock car career was taking off.

By 1964, auto manufacturers were producing the most powerful engines in racing history, and NASCAR teams picked up on this trend with Ford's 427-cubic-inch engine and Chrysler's famed 426-cubic-inch Hemi-head engine. However, with no end in sight regarding this horsepower race, NASCAR outlawed these "power plants." So at the request of Petty's sponsor Chrysler, the blue No. 43 Plymouth was parked for most of the 1965 season, and the team went drag racing.

Petty campaigned an altered wheel base Plymouth Barracuda, a forerunner of today's Funny Car. While touring the Southern United States with this car, Petty and his team learned NASCAR had modified the engine restrictions for its premier class, and Petty returned to his stock car roots, winning four races before the end of the season.

By 1967, Petty was becoming an icon in stock car racing, and by 1971, had won his third Daytona 500 as well as his third Grand National championship. In 1972, the now-famous No. 43 was sponsored by oil additive manufacturer STP. By 1980, Petty added four more driving titles to his resume, capturing the top spot in 1972, 1974, 1975 and 1979. In 1981, he won the Daytona 500 for the seventh time.

Then, in 1982, the Petty team switched from

their long association with Chrysler products to General Motors' Pontiac division, and Richard's son Kyle joined the team as a driver – the third-generation of Pettys to compete in NASCAR. Richard's last two victories were the Daytona Pepsi Firecracker 400 at Daytona and the Dover Budweiser 500, both in 1984.

At the end of the 1992 season, at 55 years of age, Richard Petty retired from competitive driving. During his final year, he was honored at each race by the fans and his fellow drivers.

He was also honored with the highest civilian award in the United States, the Medal of Freedom, receiving this accolade from then-President George Bush. Since then, Petty has been inducted into several auto racing and sports halls of fame, and has received numerous press awards for his accomplishments.

Still, Petty's most personal achievement has been the adoration of his fans. He won the Most Popular NASCAR Driver Award nine times, and to most race fans he will always be "The King."

In 1967, the race cars had big engines and real bumpers. That's David Pearson (No. 17) and Mario Andretti (No. 11) sliding in unison while Petty tries to sneak by on the high side during the National 500 at Charlotte.

CURTIS TURNER

BORN: April 12, 1924, Floyd, Va.

CARS DRIVEN: Oldsmobile, Ford

YEARS IN CUP RACING: 20 (1949–1968)

CUP WINS: 17

CAREER EARNINGS: $122,155

Charismatic is a mild term for Curtis Turner, one of NASCAR's best drivers in the early years, and one of its most problematic. He could drive anything and win. He was the first to qualify for a Cup race at over 180 mph, running Smokey Yunick's controversial Chevelle at Daytona in 1967.

Curtis Turner was the poster boy of stock car racing in the early years. This hard-driving, hard-working and hard-drinking Virginian lived his life the way he wanted and was the most colorful personality to get on a racetrack in the 1950s and 1960s.

Turner was a master when behind the wheel. He was hard on his cars and not averse to running others off the track to win a race – his nickname was "Pops," as he would "pop" slower cars out of his way.

Born in the Blue Ridge Mountains of Virginia in 1924, Turner won his first race in 1949. The victory was his first of over 350 wins, including 18 NASCAR Grand National wins and 38 NASCAR Convertible division victories.

Turner is the only driver to win two Grand National races in a row from the pole by leading every lap, which happened on tracks in Rochester, N.Y., and Charlotte, N.C., in 1950. He is the only one to win 25 major NASCAR events in one season driving the same car.

Later in his racing career, Turner was the first to qualify for a Grand National race at a speed greater than 180 miles per hour, which he accomplished at the 1967 Daytona 500.

Turner's business career was not as successful as his time behind the wheel. He was the man behind the construction of the Charlotte Motor Speedway. The concept, financing and construction were his, but when it opened in 1960, there were serious money problems. Turner did everything possible to get the track's financing in order, but he was out of his league and the track's board of directors ousted him as President in 1961.

Later that year, Turner tried to organize NASCAR drivers as a union entity. NASCAR President Bill France put a stop to that and gave Turner a lifetime suspension.

France and Turner made up in 1965, and Turner returned to plying his trade in Grand National events, but his presence at the tracks dwindled. NASCAR was becoming a professional sport with a national presence, and there was no room in it for the on-and-off track antics that made Turner famous.

Turner was an accomplished pilot. He frequently flew on business matters without incident, but then in October 1970, while flying with golfer Clarence King, Turner's plane crashed in Pennsylvania with no survivors. He was 46.

DARRELL WALTRIP

One of NASCAR's most emotional moments was the victory lane celebration at the 1989 Daytona 500.
After 17 years of trying, Darrell Waltrip won the big race.

Born in Kentucky in February 1947, Waltrip entered NASCAR's top level in 1972 at the Winston 500. He was colorful and controversial in his early Cup years, never hesitating to speak his mind – much to the disdain of the racing establishment.

Then this brash, bold youngster from Franklin, Tenn., started to put up rather than shut up. He won his first race at the 1975 running of the Music City 420 in Nashville, and by 1981 had picked up his first of three NASCARWinston Cup championships.

To keep silencing his critics, he also won the title in 1982, with another 12 race victories. He won his third title in 1985.

By now Waltrip's former nickname of "Jaws" had been replaced by "Ol' D.W.," as he had definitely earned the respect of both drivers and fans by driving for legendary car owner Junior Johnson.

Waltrip started racing on dirt with a 1936

Chevy coupe after a stint at karting. Yet, the 16-year-old didn't take to the dirt tracks, so he focused on pavement ovals where he became an ace in short-track competition.

When Waltrip moved to the Nashville area, he made a name in local Late Model Sportsman racing. He also ran a lot of American Speed Association (ASA) races in the early 1970s with this Midwest-based group.

In October 1972, an ASA race at Salem, Ind., gave the world a taste of what to expect from Waltrip. After a week's rain delay, Waltrip returned to the track and was leading one of the two 100-lap qualifiers for the main event when his transmission locked up, putting him out of the race.

He was given a ride in another driver's car for the final, starting last in the 30-car field – last in a field featuring the best in short-track racing. So not only was Ol' D.W. starting from scratch, it's getting dark in Salem, there are no track lights and race organizers figure there's no way to complete 100 laps.

"We had a quick drivers' meeting before lining up the final," recalled race promoter Steve Stubbs. "When we think it's getting too

BORN: February 5, 1947, Owensboro, Ky.

CAR DRIVEN: Chevrolet

YEARS IN CUP RACING: 29 (1972–2000)

CUP WINS: 84

CAREER EARNINGS: Over $19 million

Above left: Darrell Waltrip backed up his early brashness with a successful NASCAR career.

Above right: By 1997, Waltrip, shown here at the Daytona 500, felt it was time to step aside, which he did three years later.

Right and above: Looking quite dashing, Waltrip celebrates his 1989 Coca-Cola 600 win at Charlotte, one of five such trips to the winner's circle for that race. Teamed with the top-notch Chevrolets of owner Junior Johnson, Waltrip won the championship in 1981, 1982 and 1985.

dark, we'll put out a '10-to-go' sign, regardless of how many laps are completed to that point.

"Thence proceeds one of the damndest driving exhibitions I've ever seen and I've seen a few. D.W. passed cars up against the fence, then down in the dirt, then between 'em, you name it. He was coming like death and taxes.

"With 38 laps in, John Potts (the flagman) hangs out the '10-to-go' sign and D.W. is now about fifth. Larry Moore, the hotdog of that era, was leading. Six laps later D.W. catches him, they battle tooth 'n' nail, he goes by with two to go and wins it by two car lengths!

"The last few laps, the only way you could tell

where the cars were is by the blue flame coming out the exhausts. It was a wild and woolly affair, for sure."

Waltrip made his living racing the bullrings, and he was good at it. With some family help, he made a few forays into NASCAR in the early 1970s, and by 1975 felt he was ready to step up to NASCAR's top class. However, he knew the step would be difficult and challenging.

"Wherever I would go, I was almost assured I was going to win one or two races a week and I made a good living doing that," Waltrip said about his short-track career. "It was hard to step to the big leagues and be just another fish in a big pond. So it took some time to make up my mind that I needed to get in there, give it 100 percent, and make my mark."

Waltrip indeed made his mark. Not only did he win the three Cup titles, he was runner-up in 1979, 1983 and 1986. His victory total of 84 earned him a third-place tie with Bobby Allison on the all-time NASCAR most-wins list, and with 59 career Cup poles, he is fourth on that all-time NASCAR list.

Waltrip is also the only five-time winner of the World 600 at Charlotte, and he won the inaugural Winston All-Star race in 1985 at Charlotte. He was the first Cup driver to earn $10 million, which occurred in 1990.

Waltrip's last win came in 1992 in the Southern 500 at Darlington, and he finished ninth in the standings. He continued to race and was still competitive, but by 1996 was 29th in the standings. In 2000, his last year of Cup racing, he finished 36th.

He stayed with racing, though, driving in a few NASCAR Craftsman Truck Series events, and this led him to field a team in this division. Presently he heads up a team in this series with a Toyota truck and driver David Reutimann.

Waltrip has put his vocal powers to good use these past few seasons with the FOX Television Network as a commentator and race analyst for its Nextel Cup presentations. Aside from these duties, Waltrip owns a Honda dealership in his hometown of Franklin, and his recent autobiography made the *New York Times* bestseller list.

CALE YARBOROUGH

A more versatile driver than is generally credited for, Cale Yarborough epitomized NASCAR Cup racing throughout the 1970s.

His goal was simple: He wanted to lead every lap and win every race he entered. His career timing was perfect, teaming up with the highly respected owner and former driver Junior Johnson to amass an enviable record.

Yarborough, who started with NASCAR in 1957, may have taken a while to become a top competitor, but racing with Johnson's Chevrolets, he became a strong runner by the early 1970s and won the driving championship three years in a row, in 1976, 1977 and 1978. When he retired in 1988, this feisty driver had amassed 83 Cup victories, placing him fifth on the all-time list.

Born in Timmonsville, S.C., in 1939, Yarborough got into racing after a stint as a turkey farmer and also playing semi-professional football. His first Cup win came in 1965, and his career blossomed. In 1968, he not only won both races at Daytona International Speedway, he captured the Atlanta 500 and the Southern 500. Teamed with Johnson, he won 28

races between 1976 and 1978.

Yarborough also ran several open-wheeled Indy-car events, and raced at the Brickyard in 1966, 1967, 1971 and 1972. His best showing was at the 1972 Indy 500, where he started next to last in 32nd position, but placed 10th with 193 laps to his credit in a race won by racing great Mark Donahue.

Yarborough's last NASCAR wins came in 1985, and when he retired three years later, he had led 31,776 laps in NASCAR Cup competition, second in the standings to Richard Petty.

The former turkey farmer continued in Cup racing after 1988, creating a successful career as a Winston Cup car owner with drivers John Andretti and Jeremy Mayfield. In 1998, Yarborough was selected as one NASCAR's 50 greatest drivers of all time.

BORN: March 27, 1939, Timmonsville, S.C.

CARS DRIVEN: Chevrolet, Ford

YEARS IN CUP RACING: 32 (1957–1988)

CUP WINS: 83

CAREER EARNINGS: $5,645,887

Above left: Three-time champ Cale Yarborough gets a congratulatory kiss from Miss Winston at Atlanta in 1974. Above right: In 1983, Yarborough (No. 28) gets headed the wrong way at Talladega while Phil Parsons (No. 55) gets airborne.

GLOSSARY

Aerodynamics The science of understanding different forces acting on a moving element in gases such as air. As applied to racing, the study of airflow and the forces of resistance and pressure that result from the flow of air over, under and around a moving car. The application of this study to racing is credited with much of the sport's recent progress as teams learn more about drag, air turbulence and downforce.

Air dam The front valance of the vehicle that produces downforce while directing air flow around the car.

Anti-roll bars Bars running in the front of the car that help control how much the car tips from side to side; linking suspension parts which can be adjusted to alter handling characteristics to compensate for tire wear and varying fuel loads.

Apron The paved portion of a racetrack that separates the racing surface from the (usually unpaved) infield. The very bottom of the racetrack, below the bottom groove. If a car has a problem, the driver goes there to get out of the way.

Back stretch The straight on a circle track between turns two and three.

Backup car A secondary complete and set-up stock car brought to NASCAR races by each team, transported and stored in the front half of the upper level of team haulers. Backup cars must pass all NASCAR inspections. The backup car may not be unloaded at any time during all NASCAR National Series practice or pre-race competition activities unless the primary car is damaged beyond repair.

Balance A term that aero engineers use to describe downforce, front to rear. Balance also is used to explain the situation in a perfect world when the least amount of drag is produced for the most downforce exerted.

Banking The sloping of a racetrack, particularly at a curve or corner, from the apron to the outside wall. "Degree of banking" refers to the height of a track's slope at its outside edge.

Black box Unlike those which store recording devices in airplanes, a race car's black box contains high-tech electrical systems which control most engine functions. More technically referred to as the "engine electronic controls," the "engine control unit" or the "engine management system."

Blister Excessive heat can make a tire literally blister and shed rubber. Drivers can detect the problem by the resulting vibrations and risk more serious damage if they choose not to pit.

Blocking Changing position on the track to prevent drivers behind from passing. Blocking is accepted if a car is defending position in the running order but considered unsportsmanlike if lapped cars hold up more competitive teams.

Brake scoop Openings in the body panel and other locations of a stock car that take in air for cooling. A maximum of three scoops per brake is permitted by NASCAR officials, with a maximum of three-inch flexible hose to the brake.

Bump drafting A version of drafting in which one car bumps another. The initial contact breaks downforce and drag forces momentarily, giving the

lead car as much as 100 more usable horsepower, rocketing it away from the pack without totally breaking the draft.

Camber The angle that wheels are tilted inward or outward (the angle that a tire seizes to the track surface) from vertical. If the top of the wheel is tilted inward, the camber is negative.

Caster The angle of a spindle frontward or rearward. "Caster stagger" is the difference between the static caster settings; it affects the amount of pull to the right or left a driver experiences. The more caster stagger, the more the vehicle pulls or steers.

Chassis The basic structure of a race car to which all other components are attached. CART cars have carbon-fiber monocoque tubes, while a NASCAR stock car has a steel tube frame chassis.

Chute A racetrack straightaway, either on an oval or a road course.

Circulating Driving around a track with a damaged and/or slow car to accumulate laps and, more importantly, points and prize money.

Combinations Combinations of engine, gearing, suspension, aerodynamic parts, and wheel and tire settings which teams forecast will work under varying conditions and tracks. These combinations (also known as set-ups) are recorded and used as baseline when teams arrive at a track.

Compound The rubber blend for tires. In some series, teams can choose their tire compound based on the track and weather conditions. A softer compound tire provides better traction but wears out much faster than a harder compound tire which doesn't provide as much grip. Different tracks require different tire compounds. Left side tires are considerably softer than right side tires and it's against the rules to run left sides on the right.

Dialed in A car that is handling very well. The car isn't loose or tight, it's comfortable to the driver's liking.

Dirty air Turbulent air caused by fast-moving cars that can cause a particular car to lose control. "I got in his air."

DNF Did not finish.

DNQ Did not qualify.

DNS Did not start.

Downforce The downward pressure of the air on a car as it races. Downforce increases with velocity, or the rapidity of motion or speed. It is determined by such things as front fenders and rear spoilers.

Draft Airflow creates a low-pressure air pocket (or draft) behind moving objects. Most notably in NASCAR, drivers try to follow opponents closely enough to enter their draft and produce a towing effect. The car creating the draft actually pulls the pursuing driver who can ease off the throttle and save gas.

Drafting Practice of two or more cars, while racing, to run nose to tail, almost touching. The lead car, by displacing air in front of it, creates a vacuum between its rear end and the following car's nose.

Duct work The enclosures sealing heat exchangers, radiators, oil coolers, and so on, while forcing cool air to flow

through each. Brake ducts direct cool air through hoses to cool rotors under racing conditions. The more openings in the front of the air dam, grilles, etc., lessen the amount of downforce produced and increase drag. Teams not only control critical water-temperature and oil-temperature numbers, but can tailor handling by the addition or subtraction of tape on noses.

DYNO Short form for dynamometer, a machine used to measure an engine's horsepower and test and monitor its overall performance.

Economy run Driving slower to conserve fuel.

EIRI "Except in rare instances": A term describing NASCAR's ability to enforce its decisions when there may not be a specific rule or regulation to cover such a decision.

Engine displacement The volume within an engine's cylinders, expressed in cubic inches, that is swept by each piston as it makes one stroke downward, from top dead center (TDC) to bottom dead center (BDC). NASCAR rules require that only small block V8 engines with a minimum of 350.000 cubic-inch displacement (CID) and a maximum of 358.000 CID are allowed.

Equalize Cars in superspeedway races are required to run tires with both inner tubes and inner liners, which are actually small tires inside the standard tires. When the inner liner loses air pressure and that pressure becomes the same as that within the outer tire, the tire is said to have equalized and a vibration is created.

Factory A term designating the "Big Three" auto manufacturers, General

Motors, Ford and Chrysler. The "factory days" refer to periods in the 1950s and '60s when the manufacturers actively and openly provided sponsorship money and technical support to some race teams.

FIA Federation Internationale de l'Automobile, the governing body for most auto racing around the world.

Flagman The person standing on the tower above the start/finish line who controls the race with a series of flags.

Footprint The amount in square inches that each tire touches the earth. Larger footprints enhance tire grip to track. Four equal footprints with equal applied forces would promote great tire wear and vehicle handling.

Fresh rubber A new set of tires acquired during a pit stop.

Front clip The front-most part of the race car, starting with the firewall.

Front stretch The straight on a circle track between turns four and one. Also called "front straight" or "front chute," the start/finish line is usually there.

Gear ratio The number of teeth on a ring-gear divided into the number of teeth on a pinion-gear. Different size tracks use different gear ratios to obtain optimum performance for speed and fuel economy.

Got under A driver outbrakes an opponent on the inside of a turn and makes a pass.

Grenaded Destroyed an engine under racing conditions, usually in a dramatic show of smoke and fluids.

Greasy The track surface is slick.

Groove The best route around a race-track; also, the most efficient or quickest way around the track for a particular driver. The high groove takes a car closer to the outside wall for most of a lap. The low groove takes a car closer to the apron then the outside wall. Road racers use the term "line."

Handling A car's performance while racing, qualifying or practicing. How a car handles is determined by its tires, suspension geometry, aerodynamics and other factors.

Happy hour The final practice of a race weekend, usually late Saturday afternoon.

Headsock A fire-resistant head mask or balaclava.

Hole shot A drag racing term for beating an opponent off the starting line and winning a race despite having a slower elapsed time. Other racers use this term to describe a good start or restart.

Hooked up A car that is performing great because all parts working well together.

Horsepower The estimated power needed to lift 33,000 pounds by one foot per minute – roughly equated with a horse's strength.

Independent A driver or team owner who does not have financial backing from a major sponsor and must make do with second-hand equipment such as parts and tires. The term, like the breed, is becoming rarer every year.

Infield The enclosed portion of a track which includes team garages on most oval tracks. During race weekends, this area is usually filled with large transporters, merchandise trailers and driver and fan motor homes.

Inner liner The tire within the tire. The tires used in some NASCAR racing have a second tire inside the main tire that meets the race surface.

Inside groove or line On an oval track, this is the innermost racing line, which is usually separated from the infield by a distinctly flat surface called an apron. On road courses, the inside groove refers to the line closest to the curbs or walls forming the inner portion of turns.

Lap One time around a track. Also used as a verb when a driver passes a car and is a full lap ahead of (has "lapped") that opponent. A driver laps the field by overtaking every other car in the race.

Lapped traffic Cars that have dropped one or more laps behind the race leader after being passed by the lead driver and others on the lead lap.

Lift To raise or lift your foot of the gas pedal. Commonly used when drivers have to lift after an unsuccessful pass attempt to slow down and get back into the racing line.

Line See Groove.

Long pedal Commonly refers to a car's gas pedal because of the design. Also used to describe a brake pedal when brakes wear out because the driver has to push the pedal harder and further to slow down.

Loose stuff Debris such as sand, pebbles or small pieces of rubber that tend to collect on a track's apron or near the outside wall.

Loose A car has more grip in the front than the rear end and tends to fishtail, a handling condition describing the tendency of a car's rear wheels to break away from the pavement, swinging its rear end toward the outside wall. Drivers often report whether the car is loose or tight so the crew can make adjustments.

Low drag setup Adjusting a car's aerodynamic features to minimize drag, which also reduces downforce. This set-up achieves better performance on straightaways and reduced cornering ability. "Drag" is how much horsepower it takes to push the car through the air. At restrictor-plate races like Daytona and Talladega, you trade drag for downforce, so you have lower drag in order to have more downforce.

Marbles Rocks and debris that collect off the racing line. If a driver enters the marbles at an excessive speed, his car will lose grip and drive perilously into awaiting hazards. See Loose stuff.

Motor mounts Supports for the engine and transmission on a race car's frame, on which the motor sits in relation to the body of the car. NASCAR requires all motor mounts to be reinforced steel or aluminum, and adjustable mounts are not allowed. NASCAR teams strive to lower the motor mounts so that the car will have a lower center of gravity and handle better.

NASCAR Acronym for the National Association for Stock Car Auto Racing.

Organization founded in December 1947 by William France Sr. and others that sanctions races, sets rules and awards points toward championships for several types of stock cars: Nextel Cup, Craftsman Truck and Busch Grand National Series, among others.

Neutral A term for how a driver's car is handling. When a car is neither loose nor pushing (tight).

On the throttle A driver has the pedal to the metal.

Open wheel Formula One and Indy style race cars that are designed to have the suspension, wheels and tires exposed with no provision for fenders.

Outbrake A driver gains time and position on an opponent by applying the brakes later and deeper into a corner.

Outside groove The outside racing line. Sometimes a car will handle and perform better on the outside/inside line and a driver opts not to use the optimum groove.

Oval An oval-shaped track. Most NASCAR races are held on a track of this shape.

Oversteer When the front of a car has more grip than the rear. This is the same as a car being loose.

Parade lap(s) The warm-up lap before a race. Drivers use this lap to warm up their engines and often zigzag to warm up tires.

Parking lot After a big crash which takes out a lot of cars, the track looks like a parking lot.

Penalty box Derived from ice hockey. NASCAR's way of penalizing drivers for infractions by holding them in the pits or behind the wall for a specified time during a race after a driver was caught doing something against the rules.

Pit stop An integral part of most racing series where drivers stop in pit row so their crews can change tires, refuel and make repairs or other adjustments.

Points race The overall competition to win the Drivers' or Manufacturers' championship at the end of the season.

Pole position The driver qualifying fastest is awarded the first starting position. This means the driver will start on the inside (relative to the first turn) of the first row.

Post-entry A team or driver who submits an entry blank for a race after the deadline for submission has passed. A post-entry receives no Nextel Cup points in NASCAR racing.

Provisional starting spot Special performance-based exemptions for drivers who do not initially qualify for a race. A position NASCAR holds open for certain drivers, such as past champions, who had trouble qualifying for the race. A driver awarded a provisional spot must start at the back of the starting grid.

Push The rear end of a car has more grip than the front. This condition makes a car harder to turn into a corner. Commonly known as "understeer."

Pushing Handling characteristics of a car where its front end tends to push or plow toward the outside wall in a corner.

Qualify During designated sessions, teams must meet established lap times to qualify for (or enter) a race based on a predetermined number of spots available.

Race rubber Race tires as opposed to qualifying tires.

Racer's tape Heavy duty duct tape used to temporarily repair hanging body parts which might hinder aerodynamic features and decrease performance.

Rear roll center Located simply at the center of the track bar from the ground and center from the right to left mounting points. Roll centers are measured from the ground, but are relative to center of gravity. Higher roll centers exert less mechanical advantage, so lower spring rates can control roll or weight transfer.

Rear spoiler Two nonadjustable, aluminum pieces attached side by side to equal a rail on the trunk of the car. Spoilers create downforce to improve the car's handling. NASCAR alters the size and angle now and then to create parity among manufacturers.

Reasonable suspicion, substance Both refer to NASCAR's drug testing policy. Under it, if a NASCAR official is reasonably suspicious a driver, crew member or another official is abusing drugs, he or she may be required to undergo testing. Substances include cocaine, heroin, PCP and other illegal drugs, as well as alcohol and prescription drugs while participating in an event.

Restrictor plate An aluminum plate with four holes in it that is placed under the carburetor to restrict air and fuel. That restriction keeps the cars from reaching speeds that NASCAR considers dangerous.

Right combination Catchall phrase to describe why a car, team or driver has performed well or won a race. Included are engine horsepower, tire wear, correct weight distribution, performance of the driver on the track, the crew on pit stops and so on.

Road course A racetrack with multiple left- and right-hand turns. Generally refers to permanent, purpose-built racing facilities. Can also refer to temporary street courses built on big city streets which were popularized in the 1980s. NASCAR's Nextel Cup series includes two road racing venues.

Roll bar Large, sturdy bars designed to protect a driver if the car rolls over. Very functional in race cars but used more for style in production cars.

Roof flaps A device made to keep the car from turning over. It works like an airplane flap and comes up when the car slides sideways or backward to help slow down the car and keep it on the ground.

Running anywhere A car is handling so well, a driver can use any racing line (or drive anywhere). Sometimes, handling problems lead to a preferred line where the car handles better.

Running light A car is running with little fuel. Teams qualify with a light load to achieve maximum speed.

Sandbagging Driver who allegedly fails to drive a car to its full potential in practice or qualifying, thus being able to provide a surprise for competitors during a race.

Saving the car/tires Driving a car somewhat moderately to conserve the car's mechanical parts and lessen tire wear. This allows a driver to be more aggressive during the all-important final laps.

Scrub The amount of force exerted on the tire footprint due to the different location of tire center or pivot and the actual pivot of the spindle.

Scrubbed tires The best kind of racing tire because they've had a few laps of wear to normalize the surface.

Scuff(s) A tire that has been used at least once and is saved for further racing. A lap or two is enough to scuff it in.

Set-up The combination of settings for a car's engine, aerodynamic features and tires/wheels. Teams make continual adjustments to a car's set-up during pit stops based on driver input.

Shoot out Two or more drivers race to the end for victory.

Short track A speedway under a mile in distance.

Silly season Slang for the period that begins during the latter part of the season, wherein some teams announce driver, crew and/or sponsor changes.

Slick A track condition where, for a number of reasons, a car's tires do not properly adhere to the surface or get a good bite. A slick racetrack is not necessarily wet or slippery because of oil, water and so on.

Slingshot A maneuver in which a car following the leader in a draft suddenly steers around it breaking the vacuum; this provides an extra burst of speed that allows the second car to take the lead. See Drafting.

Slip stream The cavity of low-pressure area created by a moving object. In racing, drivers use this slip stream to draft another vehicle.

Spoiler A metal strip that helps control airflow, downforce and drag. The front spoiler or air dam is underneath the car's front end near the axle; the rear spoiler is attached to the trunk lid. "Adding more spoiler" refers to increasing the rear spoiler's angle in relation to the rear window and generally aids a car's cornering ability. Less spoiler decreasing its angle aids straightaway speed.

Sponsor An individual or business establishment that financially supports a race driver, team, race or series of races in return for advertising and marketing benefits.

Stagger On ovals, teams may use a different size tire ("stagger") on the outside wheel to improve the car's handling ability. Also, the difference in size between the tires on the left and right sides of a car. Because of a tire's makeup, slight variations in circumference result. If the left side tire is 87 inches, and the right side tire is 88 inches, you have one inch of stagger.

Stickers A new tire or tires. Term comes from the manufacturer's stick-on label denoting the type of tire, price and so on. Teams generally use sticker tires during qualifying then use scrubbed tires in a race.

Stop-and-go penalty A penalty that requires a driver to stop at their team's pit for a timed penalty before reentering the race. This penalty can be assessed for anything from speeding in the pits to contact with an opponent.

Superspeedway A racetrack of a mile or more in distance. Road courses are included. Note: Racers refer to three types of oval tracks. Short tracks are under a mile, intermediate tracks are at least a mile, but under two miles, and speedways are two miles and longer.

Taped off Usually refers to applying racer's tape to the brake duct opening in full bodied cars.

Tech Short for tech inspection, or technical inspection. Each car is submitted to tech inspection so sanctioning body officials can confirm all chassis and engine parts meet Series' guidelines. A "teched" car has passed inspections.

Telemetry Highly sophisticated electronics which transmit performance data from a car on the track back to team members.

Template A piece of aluminum that is placed on the cars to regulate the body sizes and diameters to make sure the body stays the way the manufacturer submitted it.

Tight Also known as "understeer," the car's front tires don't turn well through the turns because of traction loss. A driver must slow down entering and going through the turns to avoid having the car push all the way into the wall.

Tow-in The amount of distance the front tires are angled in toward the center of the car.

Track bar Connects the rear housing to the frame of the car and keeps it centered under the vehicle. It can be adjusted up and down to change the car's handling characteristics during pit stops.

Tri-oval The configuration of a racetrack that has a hump or fifth turn in addition to the standard four corners. Not to be confused with a triangle-shaped speedway which has only three distinct corners.

Tuck under A driver follows an opponent close enough to move into (or "tuck under") their draft.

Turbulence Rough air encountered by race car drivers.

200-mph tape Racer's tape, or duct tape, so strong it will hold a banged-up race car together long enough to finish a race.

Understeer When a car has more traction (or grip) in the rear than in the front.

Unlap A driver down one lap passes the leader to regain position on the lead lap.

Valance The panel that extends below the vehicle's front bumper. The relation of the bottom of the valance, or its ground clearance, affects the amount of front downforce the vehicle creates. Lowering the valance creates more front downforce. Also referred to as "front air dam."

War wagon Slang for the large metal cabinet on wheels that holds equipment in the driver's pit box during the race. Also called "pit wagon."

Warm-up lap The lap before a race starts. Drivers use this parade lap to warm up their engines and tires.

Weaving Zigzagging across the track to warm up and clean off tires, or to confuse an opponent while attempting a pass.

Wedge The cross-weight difference; that is, the amount of weight on the left rear and right front of the car.

Wind tunnel A structure used by race teams to determine the aerodynamic efficiency of their vehicles, consisting of a platform on which the vehicle is fixed and a giant fan to create wind currents. Telemetry devices determine the airflow over the vehicle and its coefficient of drag and downforce.

Wrench Slang for racing mechanic.

Zigzag To sharply move back and forth on the track. Drivers often zigzag on warm-up laps to heat up their tires.